ESRI

THE ECONOMIC AND SOCIAL RESEARCH INSTITUTE

The Economic and Social Research Institute (ESRI) is a non-profit organisation which was founded in 1960 as The Economic Research Institute. The Institute is a private company, limited by guarantee, and enjoys full academic independence. It is governed by a Council consisting of 32 members who are representative of business, trade unions, government departments, state agencies, universities and other research institutes.

THE TRANSITION YEAR PROGRAMME

An Assessment

Emer Smyth, Delma Byrne
and *Carmel Hannan*

The Liffey Press
in association with
The Economic and Social Research Institute

Published by
The Liffey Press
Ashbrook House
10 Main Street
Raheny, Dublin 5, Ireland
www.theliffeypress.com

A catalogue record of this book is
available from the British Library.

ISBN 1-904148-53-0

Printed in Spain by Graficas Cems.

CONTENTS

ACKNOWLEDGEMENTS

T his study was funded by the Department of Education and Science. In particular, we are grateful to Torlach Ó Connor, Pat Burke, Maura Clancy and Maureen Bohan for their support for the project. Very useful comments on an earlier draft of the study were provided by Cearbhall Ó Dálaigh, Breda Naughton, Mary Dunne and Paul Doyle. Former national co-ordinators of the Transition Year support service, Gerry Jeffers, Denise Kelly and Patsy Sweeney provided us with useful insights into the development of the programme.

We are indebted to the school principals, Transition Year co-ordinators, guidance counsellors, teachers and students who generously gave of their time during the detailed case-studies of schools.

We are very grateful to James Williams and staff in the survey unit of the ESRI for their work on the postal survey of school principals. We are indebted to Denis Conniffe for his invaluable advice on the use of propensity score matching techniques. The book owes much to comments on earlier drafts from our ESRI colleagues, Selina McCoy, Philip O'Connell, Tony Fahey, Anne Nolan and Brendan Whelan. We much appreciate the contribution of Mary Cleary, Regina Moore, Brenda Forde and Florence O'Sullivan who patiently transcribed the qualitative interviews with staff and students. Pat Hopkins is to be thanked for her efficient production of the many versions of the report.

LIST OF TABLES

LIST OF FIGURES

Chapter One

INTRODUCTION

The Transition Year programme has been in existence in Ireland since the 1970s but has expanded considerably since the mid-1990s. The programme is designed to promote a range of competencies and skills not usually emphasised within traditional academic education. It places an emphasis on developing personal and social skills, self-directed learning and providing young people with experience of adult and working life. In spite of the innovative nature of Transition Year, little is known about the way in which the programme is implemented in different kinds of school settings and about the educational careers of students who take Transition Year. This study sets out to examine the operation of the Transition Year programme using information gathered from school principals, teachers and students themselves. The following section describes the way in which the programme has developed over time. The second section outlines existing research on the Transition Year programme. Section three describes the objectives of this study while the way in which the study was carried out is described in section four.

1.1 THE DEVELOPMENT OF THE TRANSITION YEAR PROGRAMME

The Transition Year programme was initially introduced in the mid-1970s by the then Minister for Education, Richard Burke. The motivation for its introduction was a concern with the overly academic nature of senior cycle education:

> Because of the growing pressures on students for high grades and competitive success, educational systems are becoming, increas-

ingly, academic treadmills. Increasingly too, because of these pressures, the school is losing contact with life outside and the student
has little or no opportunity "to stand and stare" to discover the kind
of person he is, the kind of society he will be living in and, in due
course, contributing to its shortcomings and good points (Richard
Burke, Minister of Education, Speech to the Dublin Education
Council for Secondary Schools, 2 December 1974).

In the decades that followed its introduction in 1974/75, there have been
three stages in the programme's development (ASTI, 1992; Doyle,
1990). The first phase began with the introduction of the Transition Year
Project in 1974/75 as a pilot scheme in three schools, involving sixty-six
students. While the number of schools and students participating in
Transition Year rose in the first three years of the project's existence, no
further schools were designated as participants after 1978 in spite of a
number of schools showing interest in taking part in the project (Doyle,
1990). The restrictions on participation should be seen in the context of
overall financial retrenchment at the time:

> The Transition Year Project was initiated under the exceptionally
> difficult circumstances imposed by a world-wide economic recession
> (John Bruton, Parliamentary Secretary to the Minister for Education,
> quoted in *The Education Times*, October 30, 1975).

The expansion of the Transition Year project was also affected by the
decision of the Department of Education to invite applications from
schools interested in running pre-employment courses. Guidelines were
circulated stating that:

> The general aim of these courses is that of bridging the gap between
> values and experiences normally part of traditional education and
> those current in the adult world of work.

The first formal reference to the Transition Year Project appeared in the
Rules and Programme for Secondary Schools in 1976/77 which described it as a "pilot" programme orientated towards students about to
leave full-time education as well as those continuing into senior cycle.
Interestingly, throughout this phase, the Transition Year Project was con-
tinually considered to be in its "pilot" phase according to the *Rules and*

Programme guidelines for schools. By 1983/84, it is documented that just eleven schools were offering the programme (Deane, 1997).

Phase two, the *Transition Year Option* (TYO), was initiated in 1985 by the then Minister for Education, Gemma Hussey, as part of a wider reformulation of post-primary education. Based on a report titled *Ages for Learning* (1984) which was aimed towards rationalising "the structures within education", both the TYO and Vocational Preparation and Training Programmes (VPTP)[6] were introduced as part of a potential six-year senior cycle alongside a Repeat Leaving Certificate option. Transition Year thus became one of several options within a six-year second-level education. The Transition Year Option was intended to serve:

> . . . as a bridge for students to move from a state of dependence to a more autonomous and participative role with regard to their own future. . . . Schools have the flexibility to realise in their own way the overall aims of senior cycle with a particular emphasis on the intellectual, social and personal development of the student (CEB, 1986, p. 19).

The introduction of the Transition Year option resulted in a surge in the numbers of schools participating in Transition Year to 113 in 1986 (see Figure 1.1). It was at this stage, ten years since its initiation, that the "pilot" stage of Transition Year was formally recognised as being terminated, according to the *Rules and Programme for Secondary Schools* (see Doyle, 1990).

A review of senior cycle education in Ireland was conducted by the NCCA in 1993 which highlighted a number of difficulties with the second-level system:

> Among others, the Culliton Report and the OECD focused on the inequality inherent in our education system and its impact on the educationally disadvantaged and those with special educational needs, the over-academic nature of the curriculum, the lack of choice available to students with differing abilities and aptitudes, and the limited range of assessment approaches and pedagogical methods in use (NCCA, 1993, p. 6).

---

[6] Students could participate in a VPTP programme for one or two years after the Group/Intermediate Certificate or alternatively for one year after the Leaving Certificate.

Figure 1.1: Number of schools offering Transition Year, selected years

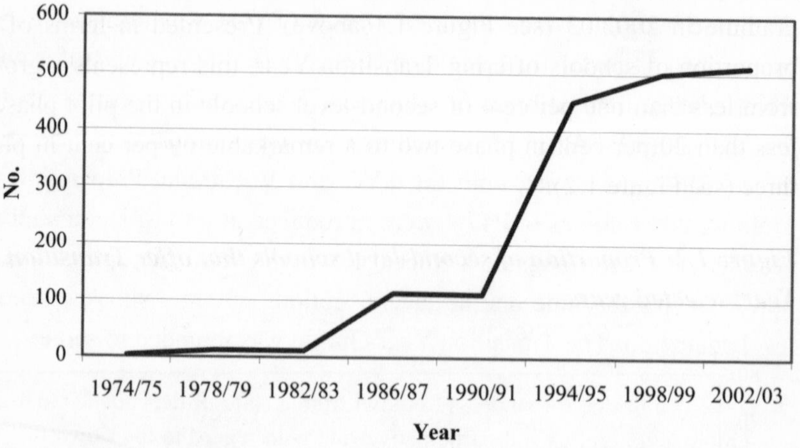

Source: Department of Education and Science, *Statistical Reports*, various years.

In the 1993 review, the NCCA put forward a suggestion that Transition Year and the Leaving Certificate could be merged in a balanced way in the context of a three-year cycle. This would allow a "transition programme" in the form of a series of modules to be taken over three years (952 hours) in tandem with the Leaving Certificate Programme over three years (1,904 hours). This proposal was not taken up but the third phase of development began in 1994/95 with the restructuring of the Transition Year Option into the Transition Year programme. The programme became clearly directed to students orientated towards the senior cycle. This is reflected in the mission statement stated in the *Rules and Programme* 1994/95, "to promote the personal, social, educational and vocational development of pupils and to prepare them for their role as autonomous, participative and responsible members of society" (Government of Ireland, 1994, p. 82) with an emphasis on personal development, interdisciplinary and self-directed learning, and providing young people with experience of adult and working life. Officially, the Transition Year Programme is now part of the revised senior cycle structure (Circular M65/00).

A marked increase in the numbers of schools and students participating in Transition Year was evident upon initiation of the revised programme. In 1993/94, 163 schools took part compared to 451 in 1994/95. Participation has continued to grow with 513 schools offering the pro- gramme in 2002/03 (see Figure 1.1 above). Presented in terms of the proportion of schools offering Transition Year, this represents a growth from less than one per cent of second-level schools in the pilot phase to less than 20 per cent in phase two to a remarkable 69 per cent in phase three (see Figure 1.2).

Figure 1.2: Proportion of second-level schools that offer Transition Year, selected years

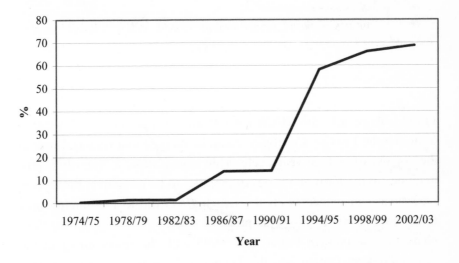

Source: Department of Education and Science, *Statistical Reports*, various years.

As might be expected, the growth in the numbers of students participat- ing in Transition Year paralleled the increasing numbers of participating schools. The number of students taking part in Transition Year has grown from under 300 students in 1978/79 to over 23,000 students in 2002/03 (see Figure 1.3). It is difficult, however, to determine the exact proportion of senior cycle students who take part in Transition Year. The number who were in the programme in 2002/03 made up 39 per cent of all students who sat the Junior Certificate examination in the previous year. However, this estimate must be interpreted with some caution as many students drop out of school immediately after Junior Certificate level with the result that the proportion of the senior cycle cohort taking part in Transition Year will most likely be higher than 39 per cent. In overall terms, while the Transition Year programme is now provided in the majority of second-level schools, it is taken by less than half of all students who reach senior cycle education.

Information is available on the gender breakdown of Transition Year students. In the 1970s and 1980s, participation in Transition Year tended to be predominantly female. However, since the restructuring of the programme in 1994/5, male participants now make up around 45–46 per cent of all participants (Department of Education and Science, various years).

Figure 1.3: Number of students participating in Transition Year, selected years

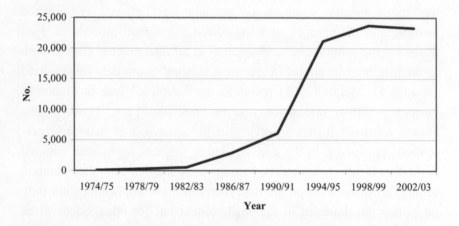

Source: Department of Education and Science, *Statistical Reports*, various years.

The Transition Year programme must be seen in the overall context of second-level education in general, and senior cycle education in particular. The review of senior cycle education currently being conducted by the National Council for Curriculum and Assessment (NCCA) will potentially impact on the future direction of Transition Year. The consultative document (NCCA, 2002) specifies four possible options for the future of senior cycle education, two of which would retain Transition Year as a stand-alone programme. The remaining two options involve combining the best features of Transition Year with those of the other programmes (Leaving Certificate (established), the Leaving Certificate Vocational Programme and, in the case of option four, the Leaving Certificate Applied programme) (NCCA, 2002). It is, therefore, timely to examine the nature of the Transition Year programme as currently implemented and the pathways taken by students who take part in the programme.

From a comparative perspective, the Irish educational system has been characterised as highly standardised with nationally specified curricula and examinations at both Junior and Leaving Certificate levels (see Shavit and Müller, 1998; Smyth et al., 2001). The Transition Year programme is, therefore, highly innovative in the Irish context in facilitating the development of tailor-made programmes and specific subject curricula on the part of individual teachers and schools. It is also innovative in its specific emphasis on personal development, self-directed learning and the absence of standardised assessment procedures. Furthermore, the programme is pioneering in an international context with no comparable educational intervention existing in similarly standardised systems. Le Métais (2003) points to the "seconde" year in France as forming a similar orientation year to Transition Year.[1] However, the French approach differs markedly in the existence of nationally prescribed coursework in the core academic subjects along with national evaluation in selected subjects. Lessons to be learned from the operation of the Transition Year programme therefore have implications not only for policy development in the Irish context but for other standardised educational systems.

1.2 EXISTING RESEARCH ON TRANSITION YEAR

In spite of its innovative nature, the Transition Year programme has been relatively under-researched (NCCA, 2002). An evaluation of the programme conducted by the Inspectorate in 146 schools in 1994/5 focused on the implementation of Transition Year across schools (Department of Education, 1996). The report indicated that the mission and content of the programme was considered acceptable in the vast majority of the

---

[1] Similar "reorientation" classes are in existence in the Swiss system which provide "bridging opportunities" to on-going education or the labour market.

schools examined. However, some concern was expressed in relation to schools where students chose their Leaving Certificate subjects before entry into the programme, the failure to develop an interdisciplinary approach to learning, the lack of on-going evaluation of the programme within schools, and the limited involvement of parents and the wider community in programme delivery. In addition, approaches to assessment were found to vary widely from school to school.

A survey of Transition Year co-ordinators indicated positive perceptions of the programme and a high level of job satisfaction (TYCSS, 2000a). However, lack of time to carry out co-ordination duties was perceived as a constraint and a high rate of turnover was evident among co-ordinators.

A study conducted for the NCCA (Millar and Kelly, 1999) provided some insight into outcomes among Transition Year participants. Their analysis indicated that students who had taken Transition Year secured higher Leaving Certificate exam grades than non-participants, with a difference in CAO points terms of 46. This difference was reduced to 26 points when prior Junior Cert performance and school type were controlled for. A greater performance gain appeared evident among students attending designated disadvantaged schools. However, this study was unable to control for other prior differences (such as attitudes to school or educational aspirations) between participants and non-participants in assessing the impact of Transition Year on their exam outcomes.

To date, therefore, comparatively little research has been conducted on the nature of the Transition Year programme, the kinds of students who take part and their subsequent outcomes.

1.3 OBJECTIVES OF THE STUDY

This study sets out to address the gap in research on the nature and impact of the Transition Year programme. The main objectives of the study are to explore:

- What kinds of schools provide the Transition Year programme on a compulsory or optional basis?

- How does the nature and content of the Transition Year programme vary across (different types of) schools?

- How do students who take Transition Year differ from non-participants in terms of their gender, socio-economic background, prior ability/performance and attitudes to school?

- How do school principals, teachers and students view the Transition Year programme?

- All else being equal, do Transition Year participants differ from non-participants in terms of senior cycle subject take-up, Leaving Certificate examination performance, school drop-out, entry to higher education and type of course taken at third-level?

1.4 METHODOLOGY OF THE STUDY

The objectives of the study necessitated the use of both quantitative and qualitative research methods. The combination of quantitative and qualitative methods has been well established in educational research internationally (see, for example, Brookover et al, 1979; Teddlie and Stringfield, 1993). However, the debate about the relative merits of quantitative and qualitative techniques and the possibilities for using a combined approach is on-going (see, for example, Anfara, Brown and Mangione, 2002; Gorard, 2002). This assessment of the Transition Year programme benefits from the complementary strengths of quantitative and qualitative information. Quantitative information was used to document the nature of the Transition Year programme across all second-level schools and the differences between Transition Year participants and non-participants, controlling for a wide range of prior differences between the two groups. However, because of the strong emphasis within the programme on the educational *process*, it was also necessary to document the implementation of the programme in specific schools along with perceptions of Transition Year among the main partners. The use of multiple sources of information allows us to provide a more detailed picture of the issues involved in the provision, delivery and outcomes of the Transition Year programme.

Three main data sources were used in the study:

1. A postal survey of second-level school principals to examine the provision and nature of the Transition Year programme;

2. A follow-up of students surveyed in their Junior Certificate exam year to compare Transition Year participants and non-participants in terms of their profile and outcomes (hereafter termed the "Schools Database");

3. Case-studies of twelve schools including schools providing Transition Year, schools who had discontinued the programme and schools who had never provided Transition Year.

1.4.1 Survey of school principals

A postal survey was sent to all second-level school principals in early 2001. The questionnaire collected information on whether Transition Year was provided in the school, whether the programme was compulsory or optional, the content of the programme, the approach to work experience placements as well as principals' perceptions of the success of the programme. In the case of schools that did not provide Transition Year, principals were asked about the reasons for discontinuing, or never providing, the programme. Questionnaires were completed by 468 principals, reflecting 64 per cent of all schools providing senior cycle. Responses were subsequently reweighted to reflect the size, sector and provision profile of the total population of schools. Information from the survey provides a recent source of information on the operation of the Transition Year programme and data from the survey are presented in Chapters Two, Three, Four and Six of the book.

1.4.2 The Schools Database

This phase of the research used a student database developed for the *Co-education and Gender Equality, Do Schools Differ?* and *Who Chooses Science?* projects containing both detailed information at the school level and student level (see Hannan, Smyth, McCullagh, O'Leary, McMahon, 1996; Smyth 1999; Smyth and Hannan, 2002 for more information). Based on a survey conducted in 1994, this database provides a particularly rich source of information on the characteristics of 116 second-level schools and over 10,000 students at Junior and Leaving Certificate levels. The sample is nationally representative, allowing us to generalise to the population of second-level schools and students in Ireland. Classes were sampled within the 116 schools, taking roughly half of the classes from Junior and Leaving Certificate levels within each school. Questionnaires were administered to all students in the selected classes, yielding a total of almost 6,000 Junior Certificate and 4,000 Leaving Certificate students. In addition, Verbal Reasoning and Numerical Ability tests were administered to Junior Cert students.

The Junior Cert cohort of 1994 was followed up to obtain information on their Leaving Certificate examination results and on their higher education (CAO) applications. These data allow us to determine Transition Year participation among those who sat the Leaving Certificate. For the purposes of the study, a student is deemed to have participated in Transition Year if they have completed a three-year senior cycle in a school providing Transition Year without repeating their Leaving Cert exam.[11] Among the students, a small number of those originally sampled did not sit their Junior Certificate and almost 1,000 students dropped out of school before the Leaving Certificate examination. Unfortunately, students who took part in Transition Year but dropped out of school during the programme or subsequently over the senior cycle cannot be identified using these data. In addition, over two hundred students transferred to another school to complete their Leaving Certificate; these students are excluded from the analysis, as their outcomes are likely to reflect the characteristics of their new school as well as those of their original school.

Of the 116 schools involved in the original fieldwork, six had been closed or had amalgamated by the time the Junior Cert cohort had reached the Leaving Certificate stage. In addition, two of the sampled schools did not provide the Leaving Certificate. These schools are excluded from the analyses of Transition Year provision and student outcomes. In sum, the data regarding Transition Year provision and student outcomes relate to 4,444 students within 108 schools.

The Schools Database represents the only comprehensive and nationally representative source of information on students' experience before and after taking the Transition Year programme. While it would

---

[11] It should be noted that this approach may misclassify students who have repeated fifth year within schools which offer Transition Year. However, the numbers involved are likely to be very small.

be preferable to have more recent information on programme participants and non-participants, no such data are available and the Schools
Database remains the only source of information on senior cycle student
experiences across a range of school settings. The data allow us to explore the differences between Transition Year participants and non-
participants in terms of their characteristics (such as parental background, attitudes to school and exam performance) before entering the
programme. This means that we can compare "like with like" in examining the differences between participants and non-participants in relation
to a range of student outcomes, including Leaving Certificate subject
take-up, exam performance, and patterns of entry to higher education.
Because students are likely to be influenced by a broader range of school
factors than Transition Year provision alone, multilevel modelling techniques were used to analyse the data and take account of the fact that
students in the same school will resemble each other (see Goldstein,
1995). Analyses of the Schools Database are presented in Chapters Two,
Three and Eight.

One restriction of the study was the fact that the data allowed us to
explore only the more academic outcomes of Transition Year (such as
subject take-up, exam performance and entry to higher education). However, a good deal of emphasis within the programme is placed on the so-
called "softer" personal and interpersonal skills. In order to assess the
impact of Transition Year on such skills, information would be required
on the skills possessed by students prior to entering, and on leaving, the
programme. Unfortunately, this kind of longitudinal information is un-
available in the Irish context. In order to attempt to fill this gap to some
extent, information was collected from staff and students in a number of
case-study schools (see below) on the perceived effects of Transition
Year on students' personal and social development.

1.4.3 Case-studies of Transition Year provision and non-provision

In order to explore the nature of the Transition Year programme in
greater detail than the postal survey of principals allowed, twelve schools
were selected for in-depth case studies. These included seven schools
currently providing Transition Year, three schools that had discontinued

the programme and two schools that had never provided Transition Year. The twelve schools were selected from the 108 schools included in the Schools Database. This allowed for the identification of schools with different student intakes (in terms of social class background and prior academic ability) along with different levels of exam performance and drop-out (controlling for student intake). On the basis of this information combined with the postal survey, three schools providing Transition Year on an optional basis were selected along with four schools providing Transition Year on a compulsory basis. On closer investigation, two of the latter schools were deemed "quasi-compulsory" since some (small groups of) students were exempted from participation (see Chapter Two). Fictitious names were assigned to the twelve schools for the purposes of our study and the school characteristics are outlined in Table 1.1 below.

In the "non-provision" schools (that is, those that never provided or had discontinued Transition Year), detailed interviews with the principals and guidance counsellors were conducted to explore the reasons behind their school's policy. In the seven schools providing Transition Year, semi-structured interviews were conducted with school principals, guidance counsellors and Transition Year co-ordinators. In addition, in one of the schools the former Transition Year co-ordinator was interviewed because of the very recent appointment of the current co-ordinator. These interviews covered topics such as the rationale for introducing Transition Year in the school, whole-school involvement in the programme, the nature and content of the programme, perceptions of the success of the programme along with contextual information on the school in general. Interviews with school staff took place over the period November 2001 to January 2002. These interviews were recorded, transcribed and were analysed using the QSR N6 software package. The "coding" of the interview transcripts allowed for the identification of common themes across schools providing Transition Year.

Table 1.1: Summary characteristics of case-study schools

School Name	Leaving Cert Performance	Senior Cycle Drop-out	School Type	Size	Social Class Mix
Optional TY programme					
Wallace Street	Below average	Average	Comm/ Comp.	Very large	Mixed
Manners Mall	Somewhat below average	Above average	Voca- tional	Medium	Working class
Victoria Street	Above average	Average	Single- sex Sec.	Medium	Mixed
"Quasi-compulsory" TY programme					
Willis Street	Above average	Below average	Single- sex Sec.	Large	Middle class
Hopper Street	Below average	Above average	Comm./ Comp.	Large	Mixed- working class
Compulsory TY programme					
Mount Cook	Above average	Average	Coed Sec.	Small- medium	Very middle class
Cuba Street	Below average	Average	Coed Sec.	Small	Working class
Discontinued TY					
Blair Street	Below average	Above average	Comm./ Comp.	Very large	Working class
Ellis Street	Average	Average	Single- sex Sec.	Large	Working class
Tasman Row	Average	Above average	Voca- tional	Large	Working class
Never provided TY					
Clifton Terrace	Above average	Below average	Single- sex Sec.	Small	Mixed- middle class
Whitmore Road	Below average	Above average	Voca- tional	Medium- large	Working class

In the seven schools providing Transition Year, structured interviews were conducted with teachers teaching the programme. These interviews covered topics such as:

- Subjects taught to Transition Year students;

- Staff involvement in curricular content and materials used in Transition Year;

- Teaching methods used with Transition Year students;

- Forms of assessment (including homework) used in Transition Year;

- Programme co-ordination and staff involvement in planning;

- Perceptions of the programme;

- Main priorities for the development of Transition Year in the school.

While some of this information was coded and analysed using the SPSS package, more detailed qualitative comments were transcribed in order to fully capture teachers' experiences of the Transition Year programme. A total of 142 subject teachers were interviewed by one of the authors, covering 85 per cent of all those teaching Transition Year in the case-study schools.

In the case-study schools, group interviews with students were conducted over the period February to March 2002. A group of approximately five students was selected per class group. In the case of one small Transition Year class, all students in the year group were interviewed. In the case of another school, a group of students who had taken Transition Year the previous year was also interviewed. A total of 88 students were included in the group interviews. The student interviews covered topics including:

- Their expectations of the programme;

- Their perceptions of the programme content;

- Their perceptions of teaching and assessment methods;

- Their work experience placement;

- Their suggestions for changes in the programme.

These interviews were recorded, transcribed and analysed using the QSR N6 software programme.

The use of multiple sources of information in the case-study schools — principals, guidance counsellors, co-ordinators, teachers and students — provided a more holistic view of the delivery of the programme within specific school contexts and provided a useful supplement to the information collected on provision at the national level.

1.5 OUTLINE OF THE STUDY

Chapter Two describes the characteristics of schools providing the Transition Year programme and the factors influencing whether the programme is provided on a compulsory or optional basis. Chapter Three compares the students taking Transition Year with non-participants in terms of their characteristics during their Junior Certificate year and explores the criteria which influence access to the programme within schools. Chapter Four describes the content of the Transition Year programme in terms of how the programme is determined, the subjects taught and the approach to work experience taken. The way in which the programme is managed and co-ordinated is discussed in Chapter Five. Perceptions of the programme among principals, co-ordinators, teachers and students are discussed in Chapters Six and Seven. Chapter Eight looks at the "effect" of participation in Transition Year on a range of student outcomes, including subject take-up, Leaving Certificate performance and patterns of entry to higher education. Finally, Chapter Nine presents a summary of the study and outlines recommendations for the future development of Transition Year.

Chapter Two

THE PROVISION OF TRANSITION YEAR

INTRODUCTION

Second-level schools differ in whether they provide the Transition Year programme. This chapter examines the pattern of provision from the mid-1990s onwards. The first section compares the characteristics of schools which provide Transition Year with those who do not in terms of their school type, size and location. The second section examines the rationale given by schools for providing the programme. Section three examines the characteristics of schools that provide Transition Year on a compulsory or optional basis while section four explores the reasons behind this policy decision. Section five examines the characteristics of schools that have had Transition Year in the past but have discontinued the programme. The sixth section examines schools that have never provided the programme.

2.1 PROVISION PATTERNS

Chapter One has outlined the growth over time in the proportion of schools providing the Transition Year programme, with a major expansion in provision dating from the mid-1990s. The survey of school principals conducted in 2001 indicated that over two-thirds (68 per cent) of second-level schools (with a senior cycle) provide Transition Year; almost a fifth (18 per cent) of schools have discontinued the programme while 14 per cent of schools have never provided the Transition Year programme (see Figure 2.1).

Figure 2.1: Prevalence of Transition Year provision

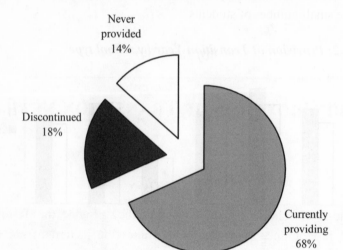

Source: Survey of School Principals (2001).

Information from both the 1994 survey of schools and the 2001 survey of school principals can be used to determine the kinds of schools which provide the Transition Year programme at the two points in time. In keeping with the national trends, provision in the surveyed schools is estimated to have increased from 63 per cent in 1994/1995 to 68 per cent in 2000/2001 (see Figure 2.2). This increase was apparent across all school types, with the exception of coeducational secondary and community/comprehensive schools.

Provision patterns in both years differ significantly by school type, with the highest levels found in girls' secondary and community/comprehensive schools and the lowest levels found in vocational schools. Transition Year provision varies by school size in both years (see Figure 2.3). In general, the lowest levels of provision are found in very small schools (those with fewer than 200 students) while the highest levels of provision occur among very large schools. Almost 90 per cent of schools with 600 or more students provide Transition Year compared to just over a third of schools with fewer than 200 students. This variation is likely to reflect the logistical constraints of providing Transition Year for a small number of students.

Figure 2.2: Provision of Transition Year by school type

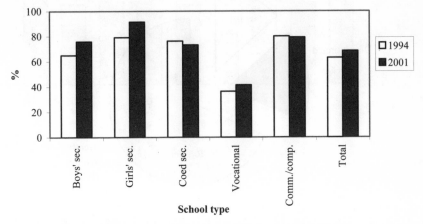

Source: The Schools Database (1994); Survey of School Principals (2001).

Figure 2.3: Transition Year provision by school size

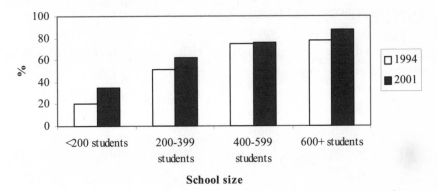

Source: The Schools Database (1994); Survey of School Principals (2001).

Provision levels were also found to differ by location. In 1994, the vast majority of schools in Dublin provided Transition Year with comparatively fewer schools in small town or rural areas doing so. By 2001, the highest levels of provision were found in all the Eastern regions including Dublin, while the North-West, the Midlands and the West displayed the lowest levels of provision (see Figure 2.4).

Figure 2.4: Transition Year provision by region

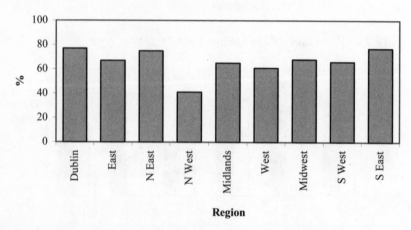

Source: Survey of School Principals (2001).

Given that school type, location and size tend to be interrelated, a logistic regression model was employed to analyse the differences between schools that currently provide Transition Year and those that do not (see Table 2.1). In addition to type, location and size, an indicator of the nature of student intake was employed: the average social class of students in 1994 and whether a school was designated disadvantaged in 2001.[1] Positive coefficients indicate that the characteristic is associated with increased chances of providing Transition Year while negative coefficients indicate that these kinds of schools are less likely to provide the programme. In 1994, no significant differences are apparent by school type when social class mix is controlled for; thus, the low levels of provision among vocational schools appear to reflect their predominantly working-class intake. In contrast in 2001, girls' secondary schools are found to have significantly higher levels of provision than other school types with particularly low levels of provision within the vocational sector. In both years, larger schools are more likely to provide Transition Year. Schools in Dublin were much more likely than schools elsewhere to provide Transition Year in 1994 but this difference was no longer significant by 2001. In addition, schools serving more working-class or dis-

---

[1] Because of data limitations, two different measures of student intake were used.

advantaged student intakes are less likely to provide the programme. In sum, school policy relating to provision appears to reflect logistical constraints (such as school size) but also assumptions about the suitability of the programme for certain groups of students.

Table 2.1 Logistic regression model of Transition Year provision

	1994	2001
Constant	1.926	1.115
School type:		
Boys' secondary	−1.230	−1.181**
Coed secondary	0.323	−1.089*
Vocational	−0.552	−2.176***
Community/comprehensive	0.105	−0.961‡
Ref: Girls' secondary		
School size:		
200-399	1.611	1.055**
400-599	2.575*	1.405***
600+	2.801*	2.308***
Ref: <200 students		
Location:		
Dublin	2.547*	0.361
Ref: Elsewhere		
Student intake:		
Average social class	−1.104‡	–
Ref: All others		
Designated disadvantaged	–	−0.929***
Ref: Not Disadvantaged		
Number of schools	108	468

Note: * p<.05; ** p<.01; *** p≤.001; ‡ p<.10

Source: The Schools Database (1994); Survey of School Principals (2001).

Figure 2.5: Timing of introduction of Transition Year in school

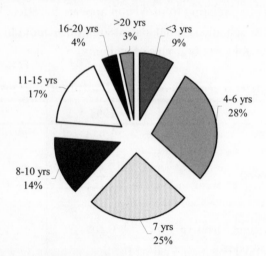

Source: Survey of School Principals (2001).

Schools that provide Transition Year differ in the timing of the introduction of the programme. The majority of schools introduced Transition Year in the period following its restructuring; in contrast, almost a quarter of schools had had the programme for more than ten years (see Figure 2.5). Vocational schools make up more of the schools that have introduced the programme in recent years.

2.2 Rationale for the introduction of the Transition Year programme

Interviews conducted with key personnel in the case-study schools highlighted some of the reasons why schools decided to introduce the Transition Year programme. Firstly, a number of teachers and school staff commented that Transition Year represented a good opportunity to provide students with an extra year in school. This was particularly evident in Willis St., Hopper St. and Cuba St. schools where students were often perceived as being too young to go straight to Leaving Certificate level:

> Well, one of the reasons actually for introducing it here was that we had an awful lot of repeat Leaving Cert students at the time. There was a sort of repeat attitude more than anything else and also the students were very young when they were doing Leaving Cert and they were quite immature. So my personal view would be that in that

year if they never did anything it's a maturing year and they're better for it (Guidance Counsellor, Willis St.).

Students being too young doing the Leaving Cert was the main reason [for introducing TY]. They were leaving school at 16 and 17. It was just too young and they didn't have the maturity to cope with the concepts that are oftentimes demanded of a Leaving Cert student (Principal, Cuba St.).

I think we felt the extra year would give a bit of maturity to students. I think most students were leaving at about 17 at that time which by European average is very young and I think a lot of us thought . . . that our seniors were making decisions about careers and further education at a time when they were still a little bit immature (Transition Year (TY) Co-ordinator, Hopper St.).

The emphasis on Transition Year as facilitating maturity was also evident in Blair St. where the programme had been discontinued. In this school the programme had been provided for students who were perceived to be too young and immature to manage the Leaving Certificate effectively:

Some students were maybe a little bit immature going into senior level. They might have maturity years-wise but may be immature in terms of preparation to follow a Leaving Cert programme or whatever. Some of them were certainly too young and I think it was seen just in terms of the overall thrust of the vision of where the transition thing was going — a chance given to broaden out as to kind of mature and develop (Principal, Blair St.).

A second reason related to the fact that some schools had had a tradition of providing a six-year secondary cycle. This was evident in Willis St. and Tasman Row schools, where Transition Year evolved from a pre-employment year originally provided in the late 1970s and early 1980s; this year had generally been aimed at academically less able students:

We always had a year when the students did a programme which acted as a link between the junior cycle and the senior cycle, as long as I can remember anyway. It was geared more towards getting young people into employment particularly in the late 70s and early 80s (Principal, Tasman Row).

> We used to have a pre-employment kind of a year. So I guess when-
> ever the government Transition Year initiative came in, it was easy
> for us because we had a year, a pre-employment year, where we
> would actually identify the students who should do it. They were
> usually the bottom, academically, group. So we had certain things in
> place then, so we jumped on the Transition Year wagon really
> (Guidance Counsellor, Willis St.).

Thirdly, Mt. Cook school decided to introduce Transition Year because it
was seen as fitting into the educational philosophy of the school, particularly in incorporating a wide range of subjects. Transition Year was seen
as a way that students could challenge themselves through new experiences:

> People are doing things all the time and Transition Year lends itself
> to that because kids have to challenge themselves. And the only way
> to challenge yourself is to get out and do things and, therefore, it
> [Transition Year] was perfect (Guidance Counsellor, Mt. Cook).

In sum, the reasons given by school staff in the case-study schools for
introducing the programme primarily related to enhancing maturity
among students. However, the existing structures and ethos of the school
also facilitated the introduction of the Transition Year programme in a
number of instances.

2.3 COMPULSORY AND OPTIONAL TRANSITION YEAR PROVISION

Schools are found to differ in the way in which they make Transition Year
available to students, that is, whether the programme is compulsory for all
students or optional for some or all students. In practice, however, evidence from the case-study schools indicates that the distinction between
compulsory and optional provision is not as clear-cut as it might first appear. This will be discussed in further detail in the following section.

In 1994/5, a third of schools providing Transition Year did so on a
compulsory basis; this had declined to one-quarter by 2001. In both
years, among schools providing Transition Year, coeducational secondary schools are more likely to do so on a compulsory basis than other
school types. In 2001, for example, 32 per cent of coed secondary schools

provided Transition Year on a compulsory basis compared to 17 per cent of girls' secondary schools. Furthermore, where very small schools provide Transition Year, they tend to do so on a compulsory basis, reflecting the logistical constraints involved in giving a choice to a small cohort of students. In 2001 54 per cent of schools with fewer than 200 students in our sample provided Transition Year on a compulsory basis compared with less than a quarter of schools in the other size categories.

Table 2.2: Logistic regression model of compulsory Transition Year provision (only those schools providing Transition Year)

	1994	**2001**
Constant	9.799	−0.305
School type:		
Boys' secondary	0.075	0.643
Coed secondary	1.593‡	0.725‡
Vocational	0.185	0.392
Comm./comp.	0.514	0.618
Ref: Girls' secondary		
School size:		
200-399	−7.346	−1.343**
400-599	−9.595	−1.270**
600+	−9.544	−1.354**
Ref: <200 students		
Location:		
Dublin	0.614	0.453
Ref: Elsewhere		
Student intake:		
Average social class	−0.846‡	–
Ref: All others		
Designated disadvantaged	–	−0.511
Ref: All others		
Number of schools	70	337

Note: * p<.05; ** p<.01; *** p≤.001; ‡ p<.10

Source: The Schools Database (1994); Survey of School Principals (2001).

A logistic regression model allows us to predict the factors associated with providing Transition Year on a compulsory basis (see Table 2.2). Even controlling for size, location and student intake, coed secondary schools are more likely to provide Transition Year on a compulsory basis than other school types. In addition, smaller schools (that is, those with fewer than 200 students) are much more likely to provide the programme for all students. Schools serving predominantly working-class populations were less likely to provide compulsory Transition Year in 1994. There is some evidence that designated disadvantaged schools are less likely to provide compulsory Transition Year in 2001, although the difference is not statistically significant.[1] As with overall provision, therefore, compulsory Transition Year provision reflects not just logistical constraints but school policy. The rationale for providing Transition Year on a compulsory (or optional) basis is discussed in the following section.

2.4 RATIONALE FOR COMPULSORY OR OPTIONAL PROVISION: "CONSCRIPTS" OR "RECRUITS"?

The distinction between compulsory and optional provision of Transition Year is not as clear-cut as it may appear. In three of the case-study schools, Transition Year was optional for all students; the way in which students selected themselves, and were selected, into Transition Year is discussed in Chapter Three. In two of the case-study schools, all students without exception took Transition Year. However, in two other schools, Transition Year was "quasi-compulsory". In Hopper St., students with learning difficulties went directly into fifth year while in Willis St., parents were allowed to opt out of Transition Year on behalf of their children, but only in exceptional circumstances, mainly relating to age or family commitments:

> There has always been a bit of flexibility. . . . You will have a student who is gone 16 plus doing the Junior Cert and the parent comes to me and makes the case. . . . Age would generally be the factor. . . . I have had cases where there was a farm — there was somebody going back to a farm — he was the only son, the father might have been ageing

---

[1] Eighteen per cent of designated disadvantaged schools offer Transition Year on a compulsory basis compared to 27 per cent of non-disadvantaged schools.

and he would have to do a term at agricultural college. And the mother would like him to do the Leaving Cert., but [the student] couldn't really afford to spend another year (Principal, Willis St.).

The decision to make Transition Year compulsory within a school was generally related to the desire to make the perceived benefits of the programme available to all students:

I originally felt Transition Year was for the select few, but I can see the advantages for all students (Teacher, Hopper St.).

What we do [having compulsory TY] is more beneficial, I think, in the long-term. . . . I think people are better prepared and more mature in terms of doing their Leaving Cert (TY co-ordinator, Willis St. school).

If you start picking and choosing I think the whole thing of just taking the good ones, that's wrong. It may be the other ones who need it more actually (TY Co-ordinator, Cuba St).

However, logistical constraints regarding numbers of students and potential difficulties with timetabling also played an important part in deciding to make the programme compulsory:

I think it facilitates the whole timetabling situation in the school from an administrative point of view. I think it is easier (TY Co-ordinator, Cuba St.).

I think from a numbers point of view, a compulsory programme is needed to ensure our numbers (Transition Year Co-ordinator, Mount Cook).

A number of staff spoke about the difficulties and issues which arise when all students are expected to participate in Transition Year. In particular, they felt that having students in Transition Year who do not want to be there ("conscripts") had implications for the overall success of the programme. It was perceived that an extra year for such students could be disruptive for the student and the rest of the class:

This school, [it] is compulsory for everybody to do it but some people will say that's wrong. That means that people who have no interest in school and, to put it politely, are not academic and couldn't care less, are held back for another year in the school. These are the kind of people that cause difficulties to the rest (TY Co-ordinator, Cuba St.).

I would hate to see it [Transition Year] as compulsory. Some kids don't want to be more than two years. It can destroy a year (Teacher, Wallace St.).

Some want to get out of school. They don't benefit from it, they don't participate (Teacher, Willis St.).

In Wallace St., the rationale for providing an optional programme was that in order to benefit from the extra year, a student should be willing and interested:

We do stress very much to the parents that under no circumstances should a child be forced into taking [TY], because what we want is willing candidates, willing students in the Transition Year. A lot of students are very much tied up with the fact that they have no intention of doing six years and students [who] would be the less ambitious students would be seeing themselves out in five years. Maybe the more content students would see themselves doing six and would be willing to do six (Principal, Wallace St.).

You get out of it what you put into it. Our best students have benefited the most, and put the most in (Teacher, Victoria St.).

A number of teachers felt that the programme was not suitable for all students, particularly those without a strong orientation to schoolwork:

Some students are not geared for it. They should be sent into fifth year if they're not geared for it (Teacher, Hopper St.).

Certain students are ready to move and get out of school. They find the extra year difficult to cope with. It doesn't suit everyone (Teacher, Willis St.).

A number of teachers also pointed out that making the programme compulsory for all students might result in losing some of the advantages and distinctiveness of Transition Year:

If all students took it, it would be like another year (Teacher, Wallace St.).

If we insisted all did it, would it lose its flexibility? If you could keep the flexibility, it would be good for all to do it (Teacher, Wallace St.).

[If] all students take TY, that would be the end of TY. It wouldn't be seen as different (Teacher, Wallace St.).

Interestingly, logistical constraints were also seen as playing a part in deciding to provide the programme on an optional basis:

It remained optional because we have a big accommodation problem (Transition Year Co-ordinator, Wallace St.).

Figure 2.6: Preference for making Transition Year compulsory by nature of Transition Year provision within the school (among teachers of Transition Year in case-study schools)

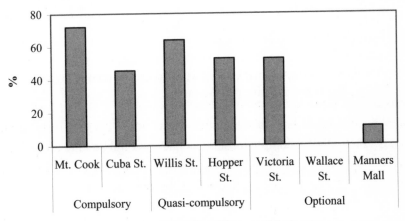

Transition Year provision

Source: Case-studies of schools (2002).

The level of support for school policy regarding compulsory, optional or quasi-compulsory provision among teachers varied across schools (see Figure 2.6). On the whole, teachers in the case-study schools providing a compulsory and quasi-compulsory Transition Year programme were divided on the preferred nature of provision. While the majority of teachers in Mt. Cook felt that all students should continue to take Transition Year as a compulsory programme, teachers were more divided on the issue in Cuba St., where a significant proportion (over half) of teachers would prefer an optional programme. Of the two "quasi-compulsory" schools, teachers were more divided on the issue in Hopper St., where half support a compulsory programme, while the majority of teachers in Willis St. felt that it should be compulsory for all students. Finally, in schools with an optional Transition Year, all teachers in Wallace St. and the vast majority of teachers in Manners Mall felt that the programme should remain optional. In contrast, in Victoria St, which had a high level of voluntary participation on the part of students, just over half of the teachers were in favour of making the programme compulsory.

In sum, the decision to make Transition Year compulsory within a school tended to reflect the desire to make the programme's benefits available to all students along with logistical constraints. The decision to make the programme optional tended to reflect the difficulties in having students who did not want to participate, the feeling that the benefits accrued to more involved students and a desire to retain the distinctive character of Transition Year.

2.5 DISCONTINUATION OF TRANSITION YEAR

Information from the survey of school principals in 2001 indicates that a number of schools have discontinued Transition Year provision. Eighteen per cent of all second-level schools had discontinued the programme, making up over one-fifth of all schools that have ever provided Transition Year. The majority of schools that discontinued Transition Year in the past did so between 1998 and 2000.

Levels of discontinuation vary significantly by school type with 45 per cent of vocational schools dropping the programme compared with 8 per cent of girls' secondary schools. Table 2.3 shows a logistic regression model which examines the factors which predict dropping, as opposed to retaining, the programme. Controlling for school size, disadvantaged status and region, discontinuation is more prevalent among vocational schools and least prevalent in the community/comprehensive sector. There is also significant differentiation by school size with higher levels of discontinuation among smaller than larger schools. Dropping the programme is more prevalent in the North-West, South-West and Midlands and least prevalent in Dublin, the North-East and South-East.

Designated disadvantaged schools are almost three times as likely to discontinue Transition Year as non-disadvantaged schools, a pattern which
is consistent with the decline in the proportion of disadvantaged schools
providing the programme highlighted by Jeffers (2002).

Table 2.3: Factors influencing discontinuation of Transition Year

	Coefficient
Intercept	−0.723
School type:	
Boys' secondary	−0.294
Girls' secondary	−1.028*
Coed secondary	−1.101*
Community/comprehensive	−1.782*
Ref: Vocational schools	
Size of school:	
200-399	−1.463***
400-599	−2.586***
>600	−3.296***
Ref: <200 students	
Region:	
East	1.445*
North-East	0.950
North-West	3.103***
Midlands	1.679*
West	1.469*
Mid-West	1.303‡
South-West	1.691**
South-East	0.698
Ref: Dublin	
Designated disadvantaged status	
Designated Disadvantaged	1.062**
Ref.: Non-disadvantaged	
Number of Schools	51

Note: * p<.05; ** p<.01; *** p≤.001; ‡ p<.10

Source: Survey of School Principals (2001).

In the postal survey, principals of schools who had discontinued Transition Year were asked the main reason for the policy decision. The most commonly cited reason for the discontinuation of Transition Year was a lack of student demand and interest in a three-year senior cycle (61 per cent). Other reasons given included the small size of the student group (16 per cent), Leaving Cert Applied being deemed more appropriate for that school (10 per cent), lack of teacher interest (10 per cent) and lack of parental support (10 per cent). A minority of schools also highlighted staffing/resource problems and the fear of increased drop-out (both 8 per cent), the Leaving Cert Vocational Programme being deemed more appropriate (6 per cent), problems with programme delivery (4 per cent), declining school size and Transition Year becoming elitist (both 2 per cent).

Three schools that had previously provided Transition Year were included in the case-study phase of the research (see Chapter One): Blair St., Ellis St. and Tasman Row. In each of these schools, in-depth interviews were conducted with the principals and guidance counsellors to explore the reasons behind the decision to drop Transition Year. This information provides a rich complement to that derived from the broader postal survey. The three schools served a predominantly working-class population area although they differed in the extent to which they drew on an urban or rural hinterland. The reasons for initially providing Transition Year in these schools were similar to those cited by schools currently providing the programme (see section 2.2 above). In general, the main reasons for introducing Transition Year had been three-fold: firstly, to benefit younger students in terms of maturity; secondly, to assist with career planning; and thirdly, to provide an opportunity to focus on personal development and a broader non-academic education. In Blair St. the Transition Year programme had been aimed at younger students:

> The extra year was to help them to mature. I would have students every year who were heading in, maybe applying for university and they would be sixteen until very late in their Leaving Cert year. Maybe sixteen actually when they are sitting in their exams would not be that unusual (Principal, Blair St.).

> I thought that a lot of students coming through the system at the time were very young and some of them were reaching Leaving Cert level or finishing school at 17 years. And we felt that they would have a

better chance if they stayed on for a year at senior cycle for a year longer (Principal, Ellis St.).

Interestingly, the focus in Tasman Row had been on more "academic" students; in this school, Transition Year participants

> . . . would be mainstream students who are definitely going to do the Leaving Cert. Now there are some of them who didn't, who have gone off and got apprenticeships and left school and so on but mainly they are in Leaving Cert now (Principal, Tasman Row).

The Transition Year programme had been provided on an optional basis in all three schools. While the principals mentioned that they had considered making the programme compulsory, they were reluctant to do so for a number of reasons. The principals in Blair and Ellis St. schools mentioned that a compulsory programme had the potential to increase dropout in the school:

> I think the feeling in the school here generally was that, if you were to force it on them, that the danger then would be that they would leave school altogether which was not what we were about because all our resources were put into it [increasing retention] (Principal, Blair St.).

> At the time our school was very streamed as well and in the lower streams their age profile was that they were a year or two older than the students who were in the better stream classes. As a result, we felt that they would leave school much earlier as a result of making it compulsory (Principal, Ellis St.).

In Tasman Row, it was felt that parents would not approve of a compulsory Transition Year:

> We did think about that [making Transition Year compulsory] but there was always a feeling that it wouldn't have been a good idea to have something that was compulsory, mainly because parents sometimes just didn't want students to do that sort of thing. They wanted them to go on straight to Leaving Cert; they didn't like the idea of them having to spend a year when they didn't particularly want to (Principal, Tasman Row).

In Ellis St., it was also felt that the provision of Transition Year should be balanced against other senior cycle options:

> And then the other reason that we didn't make it compulsory was that we have always had side by side with the traditional Leaving Cert, we have always had Senior Cert and Leaving Cert Applied. That catered as well for the needs of those students (Principal, Ellis St.).

The explanations offered in the case-study schools for the discontinuation of Transition Year echoed those reported in the postal survey. Four main reasons underlay the decision to drop Transition Year in the three schools. Firstly, there was a perceived lack of student demand and interest in having a three-year senior cycle:

> The interest just really wasn't there basically. I think both students and parents saw it as an extra year in school (Principal, Blair St.).

> I don't think there was enough interest among students. A lot of the students . . . their attitude is "five years is enough here, if I stick it five years" and then as well it wasn't producing the goods basically (Guidance Counsellor, Tasman Row).

> It is all an extra year before they get into the workplace. . . . Keeping Transition Year as a transition year, I don't see how you could give them what they want because what they would want is an employable skill and employable certificate. And while the certificates were grand and very worthy, they didn't see that "it got me office work or it got me the beautician course" (Principal, Blair St.).

In Ellis St., the process was accelerated by an overall drop in school numbers, which impacted on the viability of the programme:

> The experience here is that the numbers have dropped in the school. . . . And as a result of that, . . . there would still be between 6 and maybe 10 or 12 people from year to year who would still be interested in it [Transition Year] but the viability of that size of group is the problem at fifth year (Principal, Ellis St.).

Secondly, principals and guidance counsellors considered that Transition Year could facilitate early school leaving. They stressed that the prevalence of students working part-time in Transition Year along with having to do an extra year in school had implications for drop-out patterns:

> It was the change in attitude that happened over the last three years where it was easier to go out and get a job than it was to be working at school (Principal, Tasman Row).

> The idea of the extra year and you have this negative from some kids you get anyway saying that it didn't actually help, that it hindered them getting the Leaving Cert (Principal, Blair St.).

> I think it was the long haul in education, the money that they were earning. Then the lack of sleep, lack of concentration, lack of motivation in school as a result of it. . . . Many of them for economic reasons would work, and they would have part-time jobs, in fact full-time jobs, outside of school. And my big concern with TY is if those students went into TY they might have gone on to fifth year but a huge number of them never actually finish Leaving Cert (Guidance Counsellor, Ellis St.).

> [They became] less focused on education and more focused on this notion that we could use it as a year where we could make some money. . . . They [the students] were starting to disappear altogether (Principal, Tasman Row).

Thirdly, some difficulties were identified in relation to the delivery of the programme itself, in particular the feeling that the programme had lost focus or "drifted". In one case, these difficulties were compounded by a lack of continuity in programme co-ordination:

> It became a programme that lost its focus and I can't say that it was the Celtic Tiger or that it was the programme itself, it was a general decline in attitude towards it (Principal, Tasman Row).

> There was also criticism of the programme itself, that it had not, maybe, changed to meet the needs [of students]. The programme itself was designed five years previously, we'll say, or four years previously and because of the circumstances . . . it had lost its momentum and it had lost its direction and [we felt] that we should get out of it and stop it for the foreseeable future and not continue to try and work a system that was obviously not working (Principal, Tasman Row).

Finally, there was a feeling that the Leaving Certificate Applied programme was more appropriate to the student population in the particular
schools. This was especially evident where resources were considered to
be scarce:

> Basically when the interest wasn't there . . . you couldn't really jus-
> tify a class of five or six and the resources going into that. The ener-
> gies then went into promoting the Leaving Cert Applied parallel with
> the traditional Leaving Cert as the two options offered for students at
> senior level. . . . Transition Year finished say in June and Leaving
> Cert Applied started the following autumn. So that was it. That is
> where the energies went (Principal, Blair St.).

In sum, the decision to discontinue the Transition Year programme
tended to reflect the potential implications of an extra year in school for
student drop-out, lack of student demand, the desire to introduce other
senior cycle options (such as Leaving Cert Applied and the Leaving Cert
Vocational Programme) along with intrinsic difficulties in the operation
of the programme in the particular school context.

2.6 NON-PROVISION OF TRANSITION YEAR

Information from the postal survey of school principals indicates that 14
per cent of second-level schools have never provided Transition Year.
As indicated by the pattern of provision outlined in section 2.1 above,
vocational schools have the highest levels of non-provision with a quarter of schools in the sector never having provided the programme. Designated disadvantaged schools are more than twice as likely as non-
disadvantaged schools to have never provided Transition Year (21 per
cent compared with 10 per cent). Non-provision is somewhat more
prevalent in medium-sized schools (with between 200 and 600 students)
than in very small or very large schools.

In the postal survey responses, schools who had never provided
Transition Year attributed their decision to a lack of demand on the part
of students (32 per cent), the small size of the school (30 per cent), lack
of space/facilities, concern about the programme's potential impact on
drop-out and lack of interest on the part of staff. This information was
supplemented with detailed interviews with principals and guidance

counsellors in two schools that had never run the programme. The two schools were similar in that the principals in both schools had considered introducing Transition Year but contrasted markedly in their student profile: Clifton Terrace had a mixed social class intake and a strong orientation to third-level education while Whitmore Road had a predominantly working-class intake with higher student drop-out.

Principals and guidance counsellors in both schools were asked about whether or not the school had ever considered providing a Transition Year. According to the principal in Whitmore Rd, the possibility had been discussed but, given their existing retention problem, they were concerned about further drop-out:

> We have a problem with retention and the fear being expressed by a lot of staff was that if we didn't have a very tight, highly structured Transition Year, that we would lose more students than otherwise and also as the saying goes "it is hard enough to keep them five years, it would be harder to keep them six". They are the kind of issues (Principal, Whitmore Road).

Additionally, it was felt that by providing both the Leaving Cert Applied and Vocational programmes, resources were already stretched tightly and staff were wary of "innovation fatigue":

> The amount of innovation we have had in the school for the last few years, we have had Leaving Cert Applied, Junior Cert Schools Programme and all the in-services going with all those. We felt that innovation fatigue if you like or whatever. You know we have taken on a lot (Principal, Whitmore Road).

The Principal in Clifton Terrace had shown interest in providing Transition Year to senior cycle students, but reported a lack of demand among parents and students:

> Even last year we tried again to have the Transition Year but there was no one actually, no one at all showed any interest in doing it (Principal, Clifton Terrace).

The reasons proffered contrasted with those in Whitmore Road with parents being anxious that their children would get out of the habit of studying, thus preferring a two-year senior cycle:

> They [the parents] seem to have this inclination that it is not a doss
> year, but it is a year that if they get into that habit [of not studying], it
> is very hard to get them back on stream again to study. The usual
> comments were "well, if they're going to spend another year in sec-
> ondary school — we prefer if they repeat the Leaving Cert" (Princi-
> pal, Clifton Terrace).

The impetus for this pattern was seen as coming from the students themselves with students more interested in going on to college than complet-
ing an extra year in senior cycle:

> I'd say a lot of it is the students, they influence the parents and they
> just want to get through and go to college (Principal, Clifton Terrace).

In both schools, Transition Year was seen in terms of a choice among
competing options. In Clifton Terrace, the Leaving Certificate Vocational programme was seen as more useful to the needs of the students:

> The main difference between that and Transition Year is LCVP runs
> concurrently with the actual Leaving Certificate programme and a lot
> of it is activity based which is done in school with the teachers con-
> cerned. That's very popular and goes down very well (Principal,
> Clifton Terrace).

In Whitmore Road, given the choice between the provision of more programmes or greater subject choice, subject choice for students was
deemed more important. However, both schools stated that they would
consider introducing Transition Year if the demand was there and if the
school was provided with resources to implement the programme effectively.

2.7 CONCLUSIONS

Transition Year provision has increased markedly since the mid-1990s to
the point where more than two-thirds of second-level schools provide the
programme. The decision to introduce the programme in schools tends to
be mainly motivated by the perceived benefits for student maturity but
school structures and tradition also play a role in shaping school policy.
In spite of the expansion of Transition Year provision, access to the programme continues to vary across schools. Students in vocational schools,

small schools and schools with a concentration of students from disadvantaged backgrounds are less likely to have access to Transition Year than students in other school settings.

Transition Year is compulsory in around a quarter of the schools providing the programme, with compulsory provision more prevalent in middle-class and smaller schools. The decision about whether or not to introduce the programme on a compulsory or optional basis appears to reflect a tension between wanting all students to experience the perceived benefits of Transition Year and the difficulties which may arise from having unwilling participants in the programme. There are also logistical constraints involved in facilitating programme choice for a small cohort of students. As a result, if very small schools provide Transition Year, they tend to make participation compulsory for all of their students.

In addition to the schools currently providing the programme, a fifth of second-level schools had tried Transition Year but subsequently discontinued it. Vocational schools, small schools and designated disadvantaged schools are more likely to discontinue Transition Year than other school types. The decision to drop the programme tended to reflect concerns about the effects of an "extra year in school" on patterns of drop-out, lack of student demand and a feeling that other senior cycle programmes were more suitable for the student body.

Information from the postal survey of school principals and the case-studies of schools indicates a number of factors which shape the provision of Transition Year. Firstly, there are logistical constraints relating to school size, given the organisational difficulties in allowing students to choose between taking Transition Year and moving directly into fifth year if there is only a small cohort of students. Secondly, the programme tends to be seen as less suitable for more disadvantaged students, in part because of the risk of an extra year in school contributing to drop-out and in part because of the perceived advantages of other programmes (such as Leaving Cert Applied) for the students in question.

The pattern of Transition Year provision across schools means that some groups of students are less likely to have access to the programme than others. The following chapter explores in greater detail the extent to which students taking part in Transition Year differ from those who do not.

Chapter Three

TAKE-UP OF TRANSITION YEAR: A PROFILE OF TRANSITION YEAR STUDENTS

INTRODUCTION

Chapter Two has discussed the kinds of schools providing Transition Year. In the majority of schools providing Transition Year, however, not all students take the programme. The first section of this chapter explores the basis on which schools select students for Transition Year while the second section examines students' motivations for choosing the programme. The third section compares Transition Year participants and non-participants in terms of their background characteristics and attitudes to school prior to entering the programme.

3.1 STUDENT SELECTION INTO TRANSITION YEAR

The previous chapter has outlined that in 2001, in one quarter of schools providing Transition Year, all students took the programme. As part of the postal survey, principals in the remaining schools where Transition Year was optional were asked to rate the importance of a number of factors influencing student selection into the programme. Student preference was seen as very important in the vast majority of schools (see Figure 3.1). However, parental support and student behaviour were also seen as very important factors in almost half of schools surveyed. Teacher recommendation and student age were perceived as significant influences in around a quarter of schools. Student performance in an "entry" interview along with their academic record were seen as relatively unimportant. Principals in girls' and coed secondary schools were slightly more likely to perceive student performance as being a very important influence as were those in non-disadvantaged schools. In addition, teacher recommendation was seen as somewhat more important as a criterion for selection within designated disadvantaged schools.

Figure 3.1: Factors influencing student selection into optional Transition Year Programme (% principals regarding factors as very important)

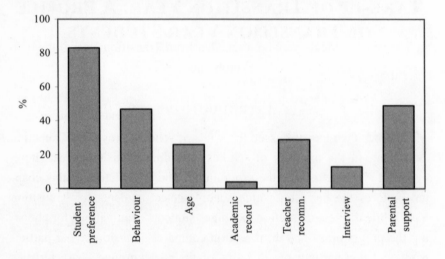

Source: Survey of School Principals (2001).

The extent to which Transition Year reflects student preference in optional schools is also seen to be variable within the case-study schools. Principals and Transition Year co-ordinators tended to emphasise discouraging particular students from taking the programme rather than refusing entry:

> [Students] would go through [an] application and generally everyone is accepted unless there is some difficulty or maybe someone feels that they might be better going into directly into the LCA or fifth year. And in that case then you know it would be talked out (Transition Year Co-ordinator, Victoria Street).

> Interviewer: Would there ever be students who want to do it but you think might not be very suitable?

> TYC: Yes, there are.

> Interviewer: And what happens in those situations?

> TYC: Usually we would find that when we sit down and explain to them the various things that it doesn't become hugely attractive to them (Wallace St.).

In addition, students who were deemed to be at risk of drop-out from school were not encouraged to take the Transition Year programme:

> If a child is very much in danger of leaving school, my own view is that they are better off going into fifth year (Principal, Manners Mall).

In particular, students may be dissuaded from Transition Year if they are perceived as having behavioural problems:

> One person in a group dynamic like that can cause havoc, particularly when you are involved in negotiated learning and that type of thing (TY co-ordinator, Wallace St.).

The potentially negative impact of having disaffected "conscripts" within the programme was also seen as a rationale for maintaining Transition Year as optional (see Chapter One). Because of the smaller student cohort in Manners Mall school, students were "coaxed" into doing Transition Year:

> Generally speaking, I think the vast majority of them should be doing Transition Year, so we would encourage all of them to do it. But . . . we would go back to some of them and really put a lot of pressure to do it because we would feel that they could really benefit from it, particularly students who were less mature (Principal, Manners Mall).

In sum, student preference was the main influence on the selection of students for the Transition Year programme. However, in some cases students with problem behaviour and those at risk of early school leaving were discouraged from entering the programme.

3.2 STUDENTS' MOTIVATION FOR PARTICIPATION IN TRANSITION YEAR

Group interviews with students taking part in Transition Year in the case-study schools allowed us to explore their motivations for entering the programme. For many students, the main reason cited was that Transition Year represented a year without exam pressures. This is an interesting finding considering that Transition Year was first initiated as a break from the "academic treadmill". A number of students commented that they enjoyed having a year with no pressure to take exams. For them, going straight from the Junior Cert exam into the Leaving Cert programme was seen as a source of pressure:

> You say before you do your Junior Cert, I am going to go on to fifth year. But then after you do your Junior Cert, you start thinking I don't think I can go straight from just finishing one exam, not even knowing my results and going straight into the next exam after that (Student, Victoria St.).

> Because I needed the break, I couldn't hack going from one exam into the Leaving Certificate. I felt I was too young (Student, Victoria St.).

Transition Year was also perceived as a break from studying for students who were tired after Junior Certificate with many preferring to ease their entry into the Leaving Certificate programme:

> I figured I would do a small bit of work in Transition Year. I would work my way up into fifth year (Student, Willis St.).

> Last year it was: Oh God, fifth year is going to jump on me now if I don't do Transition Year (Student, Victoria St.).

However, in some cases, this "break" was seen as a way of avoiding school-work and Transition Year was often portrayed by students as a "doss";

> I'm doing it because it's a doss (Student, Willis St.).

Secondly, many students expressed uncertainty regarding the subject options they would have had to consider if they went straight into the Leaving Certificate programme. Transition Year was perceived by a number of students as offering the time to make more informed decisions about subject choice:

> I wasn't sure about the subjects as well. I was thinking what subjects I wanted to do for the Leaving (Student, Wallace St.).

First student: I didn't have a clue what to do for fifth year so I said I would go into fourth year. And also because we go out on so many outings, it's a nice change because I was wrecked after the Junior Cert.

Second student: Yes, I was pretty much the same. I wasn't really sure about my fifth year choices. And all the activities, it sounded really appealing, all the different courses and you do so many different things than just normal school work so that appealed to me (Students, Victoria St.).

Finally, some students were motivated by the innovative content of the Transition Year programme, in particular, the activities, trips and work experience:

Because there are a lot of activities. You go loads of places and you start up enterprises and that seems good (Student, Manners Mall).

To do the work experience and take a break after third year (Student, Willis St.).

I thought it would have been interesting (Student, Wallace St).

While for these students taking Transition Year was seen as a positive choice, a small number of students felt they had been pressurised into taking part. This was particularly evident in Manners Mall, for example, where staff did "coax", and one student reported that "you are pushed into it".

In general, students in the case-study schools decided to take the Transition Year programme because it provided a break from exam pressure, allowed them the space to think about their Leaving Certificate options and sample a range of different activities.

3.3 PROFILE OF TRANSITION YEAR PARTICIPANTS

The interaction between the nature of provision of the programme in each school, access policy within the school and student choice shape the profile of students taking part in the programme. This section explores the ways in which students who take the Transition Year programme differ from non-participants in terms of their prior characteristics, such as gender, socio-economic background, prior ability/performance and their attitudes to schooling. Analysis draws on the Schools Database (see Chapter One) which provides rich information on Junior Certificate students prior to their entry into Transition Year or fifth year. Two sets of comparisons are made. The first relates to a comparison between students who took the programme and those who did not, including students who were in schools not providing Transition Year; this allows us to explore whether certain groups of students are more likely to have had exposure to the programme. The second set of analyses relate to a comparison between students who take the programme and those who do not in schools where Transition Year is provided on an optional basis; this allows us to explore the kinds of students who "choose" the programme.

3.3.1 Who takes Transition Year?

Information from the Schools Database (1994) indicates that among students in the Junior Certificate cohort who subsequently sat the Leaving Certificate, 36 per cent participated in the Transition Year programme and therefore sat the Leaving Cert exam in 1997. Female and male participation levels were similar so the higher representation of female students among participants indicated in Chapter One appears to be due to the higher proportion of young women continuing on to the senior cycle. However, Transition Year participation is strongly differentiated in terms of parental social class (see Figure 3.2). Over half of students from higher professional backgrounds take Transition Year compared with less than a quarter of those from unskilled manual backgrounds.

Figure 3.2: Take-up of Transition Year by social class

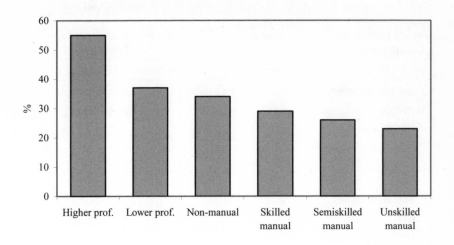

Source: The Schools Database.

Furthermore, younger students were significantly more likely to take part in Transition Year than their older counterparts (see Figure 3.3). Almost half of those aged fifteen or less took the programme compared with 13 per cent of students aged sixteen or older.

Figure 3.3: Take-up of Transition Year by age

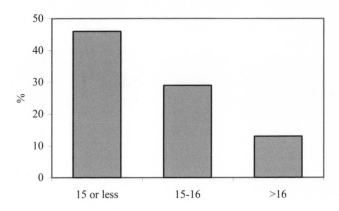

Source: The Schools Database.

Table 3.1: Transition Year Take-up: A comparison of students who took Transition Year with those who did not (all students in the sample; logistic regression model)

Coefficients	Final model
Intercept	12.225*
Pupil background	
Gender	−0.109
Parental class:	
Higher Professional	0.890*
Lower Professional	0.389*
Other non-manual	0.379*
Skilled manual	0.212
Ref.: Semi/unskilled manual	
Parental education:	
Third Level	0.291*
Ref: Primary or secondary education	
Age	−0.927*
Initial ability scores	0.009*
Student attitudes prior to Junior Cert	
Academic self-image	−0.050
Positive interactions with teachers	−0.036
Negative interactions with teachers	0.104
School satisfaction	0.044
School recreation	0.103*
Absenteeism	−0.245*
Vocational track	−0.327*
Unclear occupational aspirations	0.072
Educational Aspirations:	
Leaving Cert	0.344*
Certificate	0.420*
Degree	0.456*
Ref: Junior Cert	
Junior Cert Performance	−0.108*
No of Schools	108
No of Students	4,439

Note: * p<.05

Source: The Schools Database.

The model in Table 3.1 compares participants and non-participants across all schools, including those which did not provide Transition Year, in order to explore differences in the profile of the two groups across a range of factors simultaneously. The definitions of the variables used are giving in Appendix 3.1. Simply comparing Transition Year students to those who did not take the programme reveals that participation is strongly differentiated in terms of students' socio-economic background. Students who come from a higher professional background are 2.4 times more likely to take the Transition Year programme compared to students from a semi/unskilled background, despite taking into account differences between these students in terms of their Junior Cert exam performance and attitudes to school (Table 3.1). In addition, students whose parents went to third-level education are 1.4 times more likely than others to take Transition Year, all else being equal.

Transition Year participation is not gender differentiated but it is strongly determined by age. The older the students, the less likely they are to take part, despite taking into account differences between younger and older students in terms of their attitudes to school and Junior Cert performance.

Students with more positive views of school and a greater attachment to school life might be expected to be more likely to take Transition Year. This was confirmed in that those with greater involvement in school life through school-based recreation, such as sports and drama, were more likely to enter the programme. A student's educational aspirations proved to be a strong influence on Transition Year participation. Despite controlling for their Junior Cert performance, students who aspired to a degree are 1.6 times more likely to take Transition Year than students who planned to leave school before the Leaving Certificate. On average, students taking Transition Year tend to have more positive views of their abilities; however, the effect of academic self-image on participation is not significant when educational aspirations are taken into account. Contrary to expectations, students who report their school life as happy and have experienced positive interaction with teachers are no more likely to take Transition Year, all else being equal.

In contrast, students who have had negative experiences of school are somewhat less likely to take Transition Year. Those who have a poor attendance record are much less likely to enter the programme than better attendees while students who have experienced negative interactions with their teachers during junior cycle are less likely to take part in the programme, although the effect is no longer significant when their lower performance in the Junior Cert exams is taken into account.

Students who were unclear about the kind of occupation they wanted to go on to were somewhat more likely, on average, to take Transition Year. However, this difference is not statistically significant when other attitudes to schooling are taken into account. Students who have taken more vocational-technical subjects for the Junior Cert are significantly less likely than other students to take Transition Year.

Students who go on to take Transition Year also differ from non-participants in terms of their educational career. Students who scored higher on verbal reasoning and numerical ability tests taken in third year are more likely to take the programme, even after taking into account their Junior Cert exam performance. Raw results indicate that students who take Transition Year have significantly higher Junior Cert exam results than non-participants. However, the coefficient for Junior Cert performance in this model becomes negative and significant when educational aspirations are taken into account; in other words, the main differences between Transition Year participants and non-participants relate to aspirations and other attitudes to school rather than performance per se.

In sum, students who go on to take Transition Year differ from other students in that they tend to be more middle-class, younger, more attached to school life and have higher educational aspirations.

3.3.2 Who "chooses" Transition Year?

The analysis in the previous section is based on all students and schools in the sample. However, participation is likely to reflect provision at the school level and whether the programme is compulsory or optional. Thus, the more middle-class profile of Transition Year participants indicated in the above analysis may merely reflect the greater tendency of more middle-class schools to provide the programme and to do so on a compulsory basis. In order to control for between-school differences in provision, a multilevel model was estimated which looked at the take-up of Transition Year only in the schools where the programme was optional.

Table 3.2: Take-up of Transition Year — Optional transition year schools only (Multilevel logistic regression)

Fixed Effects	Final Model
Intercept	−2.007*
Pupil background	
Gender	0.083
Parental class:	
Higher Professional	0.137
Lower Professional	0.278
Other non-manual	0.313
Skilled manual	0.241
Parental education:	
Third Level	0.385*
Age	−1.135*
Initial ability scores	−0.000
Student attitudes prior to Junior Cert	
Academic Self-image	0.171
Positive pupil–teacher interactions	−0.133
Negative pupil–teacher interactions	−0.073
School satisfaction	0.062
School recreation	0.113*
Absenteeism	0.069
Vocational track	0.103
Unclear occupational aspirations	0.144
Educational Aspirations:	
Leaving Cert	0.804*
Certificate	0.943*
Degree	0.983*
Junior Cert Performance	−0.026
Random effects:	
School-level variance	1.702*
No of Schools	48
No of Students	2,312

Note: * $p < .05$

Source: The Schools Database.

Thirty-five per cent of students in schools where Transition Year was optional "chose" to take the programme.[2] Within these schools, there are no significant differences between participants and non-participants in terms of gender or social class background (see Table 3.2). Students whose parents had a third-level education are, however, 1.5 times more likely to take Transition Year than those with parents of lower educational levels. Older students are significantly less likely to take Transition Year than younger students. Among students in similar school contexts, those entering the programme tend to have significantly greater involvement in school recreational activities and higher educational aspirations than other students. No significant differences are apparent in relation to other attitudes to school. There is no difference in Junior Cert performance between participants and non-participants when other factors are taken into account.

In sum, students who choose to take Transition Year tend to be younger with more highly educated parents, be more involved in school life, and have higher educational aspirations than those who opt not to take the programme.

3.4 CONCLUSIONS

Student access to Transition Year is shaped by whether the school they attend provides the programme, whether the programme is provided on a compulsory or an optional basis, and, if it is optional, the kinds of criteria specified by the school for entry. While student preference is seen as the main basis for selection into Transition Year, according to school principals, it was evident from the case-study schools that certain groups of students, particularly those with behaviour problems, with less attachment to school life and those who are at high risk of dropping out may be discouraged from participation in the programme. Group interviews with students taking part in Transition Year allowed us to explore their motivations for entering the programme. Students tended to take part in Transition Year because it represented a year without examination

---

[2] Analyses in section 3.1 indicated that schools may, to some extent, facilitate or constrain student choice in terms of Transition Year entry.

pressure, it gave them time to sample Leaving Certificate subjects and it allowed to take part in different activities and courses.

The interaction between school provision and student choice means that the students taking Transition Year differ from those going directly into Leaving Certificate in a number of important respects. Transition Year participants tend to be younger, more attached to school-life and an educational career, and from more middle-class backgrounds. This profile partly reflects the kinds of schools providing the programme and doing so on a compulsory basis. However, when only those students attending schools where Transition Year is optional are examined, it is clear that younger students, those with higher aspirations, those with more involvement in school life and those with more highly educated parents are over-represented among those taking part in the programme.

The prior differences between Transition Year participants and non-participants must, of course, be taken into account when assessing the impact of the programme on student outcomes. This issue is addressed in Chapter Eight, which examines the impact of Transition Year participation on a range of student outcomes, including subject take-up, Leaving Certificate performance and entry to higher education.

Appendix 3.1: Definition of variables

Variables	Description
Transition Year	
Took Transition Year	Dummy variable where 1=spent three years at senior cycle without repeating the Leaving Cert within a school which provided Transition Year. Contrasted against all students who took the Leaving Cert in section 3.3.1 and contrasted against students who did not take Transition Year in schools providing the programme in section 3.3.2.
Student Background	
Gender	Dummy variable where 1= female.
Social class: Higher professional Lower professional Non-manual Skilled manual	Census Social Class categories based on the occupational status of parents; contrasted against semi/unskilled manual workers.
Parental education: Parents Third Level	Dummy variables where 1=at least one parent had a third-level education (either at Certificate, Diploma or Degree level).
Age	Age at end of junior cycle.
Ability test score	VRNA, combined verbal reasoning and numerical ability scores; centred on its mean value.
Junior Cert performance	Points were allocated to each exam grades; the points ranged from 0 for E, F or NG grades to 10 for a higher level A grade. These points were averaged over all exam subjects taken.
Student attitudes	
Academic Self-Image	Likert scale based on the following items: (1) I can do just about anything I set my mind to (2) I'm usually well ahead of others in my year in school (3) I am as good at school work as most other people my age (4) I'm hardly ever able to do what my teachers expect of me (reversed) (5) I'm usually well ahead of others in my class. Values range from 0 to 3.

Positive teacher interaction	Likert scale based on frequency of following items: (1) Have you been told that your work is good? (2) Have you been asked questions in class? (3) Have you been praised for answering a difficult question correctly? (4) Have you been praised because your written work is well done? Ranges from 0 (low) to 3 (high).
Negative teacher interaction	Likert scale based on frequency of following items: (1) Have you been given out to because your work is untidy or not done on time? (2) Have you wanted to ask or answer questions in class but were ignored? (3) Have you been given out to for misbehaving in class? (4) Teachers pay more attention in class to what some students say than to others. (5) I find most teachers hard to talk to. Values range from 1 (low) to 4 (high).
School satisfaction	Extent to which agrees with the statement that: "For the most part, school life is a happy one for me"; values range from 1 (low) to 4 (high).
School recreation	Frequency of participation in school-organised sports and extracurricular activities (such as plays, debates etc.) in the previous two weeks; values range from 0 (low) to 4 (high).
Absenteeism	Dummy variable where 1 = pupil has poor/average attendance over the previous year; contrasted against good attendance.
Vocational subjects	Dummy variable where 1 = took two or more vocational subjects (Materials Technology, Metalwork, Technical Graphics and Home Economics) at Junior Cert.
Unclear occupational aspirations	Dummy variable where 1 = no clear occupational preference at age 14.
Educational aspirations	Set of dummy variables where 1 = aspire to Leaving Cert, Cert/Diploma and Degree qualifications respectively.

Chapter Four

CONTENT OF THE TRANSITION YEAR PROGRAMME

INTRODUCTION

The Transition Year programme allows for flexibility at the school level to develop a programme encompassing a range of subjects and activities not usually incorporated into second-level education. The Department of Education and Science specifies certain curriculum principles underlying the Transition Year programme:

> Curriculum content is a matter for selection and adaptation by the individual school having regard to these guidelines, the requirements of pupils and the views of parents (Department of Education, 1993).

Information from the postal survey of school principals along with detailed case-studies of provision in seven schools allow us to explore the content of the Transition Year programme in different school contexts. The second section of the chapter examines the way in which the content of the programme is decided in schools. The third section relates to the timing and approach to subject choice. Section four discusses the content of the programme across different schools while highlighting the variation in the provision of "academic" subjects as part of Transition Year. The role of work experience within Transition Year is discussed in section five while career guidance provision for Transition Year students is outlined in section six. The chapter begins by placing programme content within the context of the objectives of the Transition Year programme.

4.1 OBJECTIVES OF TRANSITION YEAR

The objectives of Transition Year are outlined in a number of Department documents and circulars. Broadly, the mission is seen as designed:

> to promote the personal, social, educational and vocational development of pupils and to prepare them for their role as autonomous, participative and responsible members of society (Department of Education, 1993).

According to the Transition Year Curriculum Support Service (TYCSS) guidelines, the aims of Transition Year are inter-related and interdependent and should be strongly reflected in every Transition Year programme. The programme has three main aims:

1. Education for maturity with the emphasis on personal development, including social awareness and increased social competence;

2. The promotion of general, technical and academic skills with an emphasis on interdisciplinary and self-directed learning;

3. Education through experience of adult working life as a basis for personal development and maturity.

According to the guidelines, the aims and mission of Transition Year should permeate the entire school. In order for the programme to be a success, it is recommended that schools providing the programme take responsibility for setting appropriate goals and defining the objectives necessary for their achievement.

In order to investigate the formulation of the programme objectives at school level, in the postal survey principals were asked to rank the possible objectives of the Transition Year programme.[4] Interestingly, the personal development and maturity of the student were seen as the most important objectives followed by the development of social skills among students (see Figure 4.1). Promoting academic performance, subject and

---

[4] The specified objectives stated were personal development, social skills development, academic performance, career awareness, maturity, civic awareness and subject awareness.

career awareness, and civic awareness were seen as much less important objectives by school principals.

Figure 4.1: Perceived importance of the objectives of the Transition Year programme

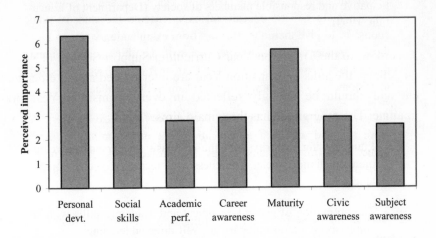

Source: Survey of School Principals (2001).

In-depth interviews with principals, co-ordinators and teachers indicated that the objectives of the programme had been taken on board by staff. The role of Transition Year in promoting student maturity was emphasised in all of the schools studied:

> I would think it [the objective of TY] would be to allow them to mature and develop emotionally and intellectually and socially (Guidance Counsellor, Manners Mall).

> [The objectives] we talk about are confidence, [becoming] broad-minded, working at motivation, working with others, [being] more aware of what's going on in this world and then the academics (Principal, Cuba St.).

> [The objectives of Transition Year are] . . . to develop confidence, resourcefulness, a new alternative to study skills. The year worked really well, [the students were] a lot more focused in fifth and sixth years. You could pick out those who've done it. By fifth year they're

> more relaxed, grown up, get to know where things are coming from (Teacher, Manners Mall).

The emphasis within Transition Year is on a more holistic view of education rather than a focus on academic work:

> I think the main objective of Transition Year in the school is to give a much more holistic educational experience to the students who choose it, to give them the year out from examination work, to give them a broader educational experience with the ultimate aim of them doing much better in their Leaving Cert, first of all from a personal development point of view (Guidance Counsellor, Wallace St.).

> To give them a bridge between Junior Cert and Leaving Cert. A more rounded approach to education, not just homework based, things apart from academic things, like project work. A lot comes from them — they're responsible for their own education (Teacher, Mt. Cook).

The facilitation of self-directed learning and the development of independent study skills were also highlighted:

> [It is] to get students directing their own learning and to develop some of the skills needed for Leaving Certificate . . . maybe to introduce some of the Leaving Certificate topics (Teacher, Hopper St.).

> [It is to] introduce courses and material not normally on the school curriculum, foster independent study, work experience, give a breather from the grind of the points race (Teacher, Cuba St.).

> It helps them to mature, it has helped them to think more independently (Teacher, Willis St.).

> [It is] to create interest in learning. To develop the research skills of pupils by giving them projects and getting the students doing research. To develop pupils' self-esteem and self-confidence, like getting pupils working in groups and each person's talents being used in the overall project (Teacher, Mt. Cook).

Finally, an increase in awareness of subject and career opportunities, particularly through exposure to working life, was also a central objective among teachers and principals in the case-study schools:

> It gives them time to experience a few more options to explore and I
> think the work experience module there certainly sets them thinking,
> it sets them up (Guidance Counsellor, Victoria St).

The survey of principals revealed little variation across school types in
their reported objectives. However, there was a slight tendency for com-
munity/comprehensive and boys' schools along with schools with compulsory Transition Year to see academic performance as a more important objective than other school types. Furthermore, evidence from the
case-study schools indicated that the most important objectives of Transition Year related not to the type of school per se but rather to the nature
of the student intake. This was evident in Willis St., Hopper St. and
Manners Mall, schools with very different intakes. Willis St. was more
middle-class in profile with a strong orientation to higher education. The
principal saw Transition Year as focused on developing students' maturity while, at the same time, maintaining academic standards among the
group:

> I suppose they [the objectives] are two-fold. A very high number of
> our students go on to third level and the extra year maturity helps
> them. We would have the usual type of things in TY. . . . A bit of
> work experience shows them the world of work, then we would de-
> vise a programme which we try to balance [with] . . . the academic
> year. I believe you don't withdraw them entirely from the academic
> world (Principal, Willis St.).

In contrast, in Manners Mall, a school with a more disadvantaged student
population, the fostering of maturity was seen as a central aim, with the
emphasis on providing students with a range of opportunities they may
not otherwise access:

> The main objective of the programme is maturity and that the stu-
> dents would grow in a lot of different ways. We are designated dis-
> advantaged and a lot of our students would come from, what I
> wouldn't call just socially disadvantaged homes, culturally disadvan-
> taged homes. . . . I would feel that they would be disadvantaged in
> ways that middle-class children [are not]. And we would hope in TY
> to expose them to experiences that . . . a child from a better-off home
> would be exposed to. And to broaden their horizons basically (Prin-
> cipal, Manners Mall).

In Hopper St., Transition Year was seen as an opportunity to reinforce academic achievement (in the context of a broader education) among their particular students:

> This would be a lower middle to sort of working-class clientele —
> that would be the main kind of background. In terms of the pupils of
> the school, their aspirations would be less than they should be. The
> kids in the main would be fairly average ability but . . . (to use an
> old-fashioned phrase) they would lack ambition. And I see the pro-
> gramme particularly then that it gives three years to do some section
> of the Leaving Cert. and enable them to get a certain level in the
> Leaving Cert. That's one strand of it (Principal, Hopper St.).

The remainder of the chapter, along with Chapter Five, outlines how the objectives of the Transition Year programme are operationalised in terms of the content and management of the programme.

4.2 PROGRAMME DESIGN AND DEVELOPMENT

This section draws on interviews with school management, guidance counsellors, Transition Year co-ordinators and subject teachers to inves- tigate how the Transition Year programme and curriculum is designed, a process which ultimately dictates what subjects are offered to Transition Year students. Departmental guidelines suggest that curriculum content is a matter for selection and adaptation by the individual school in accor- dance with the requirements of students, the views of parents, the possi- bilities offered by employers, and wider community interests. This flexi- bility is itself likely to result in variation in the content and breadth of Transition Year programmes across schools (see below).

4.2.1 Programme content

The case-study schools varied in the extent to which subject teachers felt they were involved in shaping the content of the Transition Year pro- gramme and the specific subject they taught. In Hopper St., the initial programme was designed by a core team of teachers:

> I suppose there was a lot of discussion and a lot of teachers got in-
> volved when the programme started off, and each subject area de-

vised its own programme and there was a day given to design modules and different areas (Principal, Hopper St.).

However, at the time of the fieldwork, two-thirds of the teachers interviewed in this school felt they had not been involved in programme design with the decision about programme content seen as "top-down":

> The principal decides on what subjects are offered (Teacher, Hopper
> St.).

A similar situation was evident in Manners Mall, albeit in the context of
some consultation with staff:

> Well it was decided originally between the co-ordinator and the staff,
> I suppose slightly on an ad hoc basis. The principal, deputy principal,
> the co-ordinator would have decided but there would have been an
> input from staff as well (Principal, Manners Mall).

Despite the fact that the majority of teachers in Victoria St. felt that they
were not involved in deciding what subjects or modules are offered,
good communications among Transition Year teachers and school management contributed to a considerable degree of co-operation among
those teaching the programme:

> They [teachers] are professional people and they know what they are
> at. Between us all there is a core group that are there most of the
> time. It's a bit of interaction between us all. If somebody has some-
> thing new they'll come to me with it and we'll discuss it or whatever.
> We discuss things like that (Principal, Victoria St.).

Teachers in Willis St. and Mt. Cook felt that they were somewhat involved in programme design with the main decisions being made by a
core team of teachers:

> Well, it's usually the year head and the art teacher is on it this year
> for some reason. I mean I think again the makeup of the team — I
> think I'm on it as the year leader, the co-ordinator, the year head and
> then whoever happens to be free that's teaching Transition Year
> (Guidance Counsellor, Willis St.).

However, within this framework, individual teachers had suggested particular subjects and these had been taken on board:

> We submitted a programme at the beginning and then it was chosen (Teacher, Willis St.).

> Italian was pushed by me for those not doing French or German (Teacher, Willis St.).

In contrast, the majority of teachers in Cuba St. and Wallace St. indicated that they were the main person involved in deciding to offer their subject and it was open to teachers to suggest ideas for subjects to other staff members:

> It was almost self-selecting from the actual subject areas so the different subject areas would have met initially here and decided on the curriculum and then the teachers emerged from that. The individual teachers have honed it down and varied it over the years (Principal, Wallace St.).

> Getting feedback from the teachers, meeting with them individually and then generally there is a staff meeting when it is one of the items on the agenda when people will make suggestions to say "Can we do this or can we do that?" (Principal, Cuba St.).

> The Principal is very flexible. I mean we can introduce new courses and stuff (Guidance Counsellor, Cuba St.).

A recurring theme in the interviews indicated the importance of availability of subject teachers. In Mt. Cook, provision is seen as dependent on teacher availability and willingness to offer particular subjects:

> At the start it would have been whatever the teachers were prepared to offer and I suppose that is carried on. We actually ask the teachers what they are prepared to offer the following year and then it becomes a timetabling thing as to what the best balance is (Transition Year Co-ordinator, Mt. Cook).

This pattern was replicated in a number of other schools:

> When we put the whole package together, sometimes there is either no place for something or there is a hole to be filled and so [we] let

the word go out — if somebody is interested in doing something, picking up on an area or I might even approach an individual teacher (Principal, Cuba St.).

I suppose really the subjects that are done were selected as I suppose originally based on what teacher subjects were available because I know one of the ones who does media studies but maybe not all schools do it (TY Co-ordinator, Victoria St.).

It depends on personnel — you know you can offer a subject if you have somebody who can teach it. But if you haven't . . . You know it is dictated a little bit as well by the teachers who are available in this school (Principal, Manners Mall).

This ultimately means that if there is a lack of staff in any of the subject areas, then a subject may not be offered to Transition Year students.

Interviews with management and teachers emphasised the importance of the programme evolving over time as result of on-going evaluation:

None of the courses have been stagnant. They have all evolved to a certain extent (Guidance Counsellor, Cuba St.).

The overall programme evolves actually. It has evolved over a period of years I suppose and we would look at the programme occasionally, identify shortcomings and shortfalls and try to do something about those (Guidance Counsellor, Willis St.).

Whatever had worked well we have kept and things that haven't worked well we have dropped. . . . Every year we look at it to see is this what we should be doing next year. I feel what we are doing now seems to have . . . settled fairly well and be very satisfactory. But again we will make little changes (Principal, Manners Mall).

A number of guidance counsellors and school management commented on how the evolving nature of Transition Year subjects contributes to a "balanced" approach in subject provision between the continuation of a number of core academic subjects and other more "innovative" Transition Year subjects:

Well, we would have had a Transition Year co-ordinator for years and it sort of developed, evolved, balancing the content with the rest of the programme. It sort of evolved. It wasn't something where we put 60 per cent curriculum and 40 per cent extra-curricular, it just found its own level (Guidance Counsellor, Mt. Cook).

You've got subject teachers having the opportunity to do other things within the context of their subject and developing that and then people with particular interests offering those as modules or curricular activities in the context of Transition Year. Then you have the basic structure of the programme in terms of the class week (Principal, Mt. Cook).

In sum, the case-study schools were found to vary in the extent to which subject teachers were involved in the design of the Transition Year programme. Programme content also reflected logistical constraints in terms of the availability of teachers for specific subjects. Programme content was not seen as fixed but changed over time in response to perceived needs.

4.2.2 Subject content within Transition Year

There was less variation among teachers in the extent to which they felt involved in deciding the content of their particular subject for Transition Year than in deciding the overall programme. The majority of teachers in all schools, with the exception of Hopper St., described themselves as the main person or very involved in deciding subject content. The pattern in Hopper St. reflects the importance of groupings of subject teachers in deciding a common course content:

Deciding the subject and the module is not applicable. We decided as a group at the start that the year had to become structured. We got together, the head of department and other teachers, to do the content and the materials and textbooks used (Teacher, Hopper St.).

However, co-operation among groups of teachers in shaping course content was also evident in particular subjects in the other schools:

The content would have been decided at subject meetings among all of the teachers of that particular subject. Now that would have happened back at the very start (TY Co-ordinator, Wallace St.).

> All English teachers have a meeting at the start of each year to de-
> cide the content of the course (Teacher, Willis St.).

Some continuity with the kinds of courses developed by teachers who
had previously taught the programme is also evident:

> We are influenced by those who took it before (Teacher, Manners
> Mall).

> I wasn't teaching when it [TY] was introduced. It [the course] was
> drawn up by two other tutors (Teacher, Victoria St.).

In general, teachers in the case-study schools decide their own subject
content within the context of the overall Transition Year programme.
However, in some instances, course content is decided at the level of
subject departments.

4.3 TIMING AND NATURE OF SUBJECT CHOICE: IS TIMING EVERYTHING?

The report on the Inspectorate evaluation of Transition Year (1996) expressed concern about a minority of schools in which students were required to select their Leaving Certificate subjects before entry to Transition Year. According to the TYCSS (2000a), such practice is seen as
contrary to programme innovation, communicates an unwelcome examination orientation to the year and denies students the opportunity which
Transition Year should afford to reflect on their future. Guidelines currently recommend that students choose their Leaving Certificate subjects
at the end of Transition Year and that the programme should be used to
expose students to a range of different subjects in order to enhance their
later choice.

4.3.1 Timing of subject choice

Results from the survey of school principals indicate that just six per
cent of schools require students to choose their Leaving Certificate subjects before, or in the first term of, Transition Year. Early choice is
somewhat more prevalent in boys' secondary schools (15 per cent of this
group) and in schools where Transition Year was compulsory (20 per

cent of these schools compared with 1 per cent of schools where the programme is optional).

Two of the case-study schools in this study, Victoria and Wallace St., require students to choose Leaving Certificate subjects in the second term of Transition Year while the choice is made in the last term in the five other schools. Later choice is seen as providing students with the opportunity to "sample" different subjects and thus provide a more informed basis for selecting Leaving Cert subjects:

> It's too important to get the right subjects. If they're comfortable with the subjects then I'm happy and there're no problems and they work and they study and their future opens up because they are obviously going to do better knowing that the subjects they have chosen are ones that they are happy and comfortable with (Guidance Counsellor, Mt. Cook).

> It gives them time to study themselves and see what subjects they actually want. I think coming into third year they are focussing on Junior Cert and usually they are very focused on the subjects and that may not be the best. I think they really do need a bit of time that Transition Year gives them (Guidance Counsellor, Victoria St.).

> I would say a lot of them have a lot of their minds made up before they take Transition Year but they are not sure. And in a lot of cases it would . . . make their minds up for them. And I would say maybe about 25 per cent of students would try a subject they never tried before as a result of Transition Year (TY Co-ordinator, Wallace St.).

In overall terms, early subject choice, that is, the selection of Leaving Certificate subjects before entry to Transition Year, does not appear to be a problem across second-level schools. This occurs in only a very small number of schools providing Transition Year. The opportunity to try different subjects within Transition Year is seen as contributing to a more informed choice of Leaving Cert subjects on the part of students.

4.3.2 The nature of subject choice within Transition Year

As well as differing in their approach to the choice of Leaving Certificate subjects, schools can vary in the degree to which they provide a choice of subjects or modules within Transition Year itself. Schools can provide the same "core" subjects to all Transition Year students or alternatively allow students a degree of subject choice with "optional" subjects as well as the specified "core". In under a third of schools, all Transition Year students take the same core subjects, with seventy per cent of schools offering both core and optional subjects/modules to students. The provision of subject choice within Transition Year does not vary by school sector, school size or disadvantaged status. However, schools where Transition Year is optional are more likely to have core subjects only; in over one-third of schools with optional Transition Year, all students take the same subjects compared with just over a tenth of schools with a compulsory programme. This is likely to reflect the logistical constraints in providing subject choices in schools where Transition Year is taken by a smaller cohort of students.

Among schools providing core subjects only, the average number of subjects provided is 16.5. Girls' secondary and community/comprehensive schools provide significantly more subjects than the other school types. In addition, larger schools tend to provide more subjects, although the variation is not significant. Fewer subjects are provided in designated disadvantaged schools than in their non-disadvantaged counterparts. The pattern of subject provision by school type and size is consistent with that found for junior cycle subjects (see Smyth et al., 2004); in other words, schools which provide a greater number of subjects in general tend to provide more subjects to Transition Year students. Among schools providing both core and optional subjects, students take an average of 13 core subjects with an average of 9 subjects provided on an optional basis.

Among the case-study schools, six of the schools have both core and optional subjects while one school, Victoria St., although offering students a choice of European languages, has core subjects only. This policy was perceived as reflecting logistical constraints within a particular year. Students themselves reported that the large numbers in Transition Year led to timetabling constraints which contributed to the lack of subject choice. While students in this school were disappointed that they did not have a choice, they were very understanding of the situation, indicating a good relationship with teachers:

> But that was only this year because there were so many of us and the
> co-ordinators changed so there was big confusion but next year they
> will have it [subject choice] organised (Student, Victoria St.).

Although students in the school were positive about the programme (see
Chapter Seven), the lack of subject choice meant that academic courses
were seen as little different from those at junior cycle level:

> Like academic-wise, I suppose that nothing really changed much but
> like sports and PE and trips, that's the good part (Student, Victoria
> St.).

Among the schools which offered both core and optional subjects, the
approach to subject choice varied. In Victoria St., Manners Mall, Mt.
Cook and Hopper St., students tended to select subjects which they pur-
sued for the whole school year. However, in Cuba St., Wallace and
Willis St. schools, subjects were "blocked" with students taking groups
of subjects for part of the year (for example, a term). The subjects offered in blocks tended to be more innovative subjects (such as third-level
taster subjects) rather than traditional academic subjects.

The following section outlines the kinds of subjects provided and the
subject areas or "layers" covered across different schools.

4.4 SUBJECT "LAYERS" WITHIN TRANSITION YEAR

The kinds of Transition Year subjects offered vary greatly from school to
school, a characteristic which is associated with the curricular flexibility
of the Transition Year programme. The guidelines recommend a balanced approach in subject provision between continuation of a number of
core academic subjects (most commonly Irish, English, Maths and a
European language), a sampling of subjects not generally provided by
the school, a variety of courses designed to broaden students' horizons
and some modules and activities specifically aimed at promoting the objectives of Transition Year. However, to date little has been known about
the actual content of the Transition Year programme across all schools.

Table 4.1: Knowledge areas within Transition Year

Category	Description	Examples
Academic subjects	Subjects traditionally provided either at Junior Cert or Leaving Cert level	Irish, English, Maths, Science
Third-level taster subjects	Introduction to subjects that might be studied at third-level	Law, Media Studies, Journalism, Archaeology, Film Studies, Media Studies
Personal development	Any course focusing on personal/social development or health education	Health Education, Personal Development, Grooming
Sports/leisure activities	Any sports or leisure courses, including adventure sports	Football, GAA Coaching, Sailing, Swimming, PE
Cultural studies	Any arts or creative subjects	Art, Craft, Fashion Design, Drama Workshop, Music, Dance
IT studies	Any computer-related courses (including software)	European Computer Driver Licence (ECDL), Computer Programming, Key Board Skills
Civic/social studies	Including voluntary or charity work, community action programmes	Community action, African links
Work-related learning	Exposure to world of work	Work experience (where mentioned as a subject), Mini-Companies, Enterprise Education, Career Guidance, Visits to Employers and Universities
Practical skills	Any "hands-on" skills	Driving, flower arranging
Other skills/activities	Any other activities specifically mentioned	Guest speakers, school trips, competitions such as the Young Scientist and Entrepreneurship

Within the postal survey, school principals were asked to list the core and optional subjects offered to Transition Year students in their school. Because of the diversity of subjects named, the subjects were grouped into the following categories; academic (that is, traditional second-level subjects), third-level taster (academic subjects more commonly provided at third-level), personal development, sports and leisure, cultural, computer/IT studies, civic/social awareness subjects, practical skills, work-related learning and other skills/activities. The definitions of these categories are given in Table 4.1. This classification of courses covers all recommended "layers" or knowledge areas of the Transition Year Programme.

Figure 4.2: Proportion of schools offering the various "layers" of the Transition Year Programme

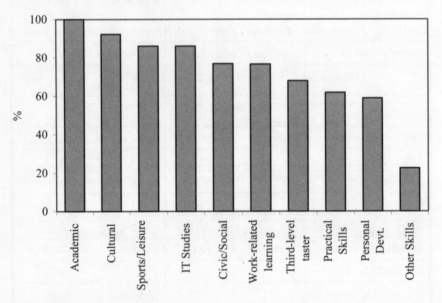

Source: Survey of School Principals (2001).

The average number of subject areas or "layers" provided within the Transition Year programme is seven. Figure 4.2 indicates the proportion of schools offering each of the knowledge areas either as core or optional subjects. Six subject areas can be seen as forming the nucleus of the Transition Year programme as they are provided in the vast majority of schools surveyed: Academic, Cultural Studies, Sports and Leisure, IT

Studies, Civic/Social Studies and Work-related learning. In contrast, much lower levels of provision are found for third-level taster subjects and personal development studies than might be expected given the nature of Transition Year. However, it should be noted that other subjects may be used to foster personal development rather than it forming a separate timetabled subject. Allowing students a choice of subjects enables schools to offer a wider range of subject areas. While all schools offer academic subjects, each of the other subject areas has a higher level of provision in schools where Transition Year subjects are offered on both a compulsory and optional basis (see Table 4.2). In particular, considerably higher levels of third-level taster subjects and practical skills are evident in schools which provide both core and optional subjects than in schools without subject choice.

Table 4.2: Proportion of schools offering the various Transition Year subject areas

Discipline	% Total	% Core	% Core and Optional
Academic subjects	100	100	100
Cultural subjects	92.3	87.8	94.1
Sports & Leisure	86.1	78.6	90.4
IT Studies	86.1	84.0	86.6
Civic/Social Studies	76.9	73.5	78.2
Work-Related Learning	76.6	72.4	78.2
Third-Level taster	68.0	61.2	70.7
Practical Skills	61.8	43.9	69.0
Personal Development	58.9	54.0	60.3
Other Skills	22.5	11.2	26.8
Total	**333**	**98**	**235**

Source: Survey of School Principals (2001).

There is regularity across schools in the presence of a nucleus of six subject areas: academic subjects, cultural studies, sports/leisure, IT studies, civic/social studies and work-related learning. This regularity is apparent across schools from different sectors, schools of different sizes and disadvantaged and non-disadvantaged schools (see Appendix Tables A4.1 to A4.4). However, some variation in provision is apparent. The time-tabling of civic/social studies is significantly influenced by school type; these subjects are provided in the vast majority (88 per cent) of girls' secondary schools compared with over three quarters of community/comprehensive and boys' secondary schools and 68 per cent of coed secondary and vocational schools (Table A4.1). Third-level taster courses and IT studies are more likely to be provided in very large schools than in smaller schools (Table A4.2). Furthermore, a signifi-cantly lower proportion of disadvantaged schools timetable civic/social studies and third-level taster subjects (67 per cent and 53 per cent respec-tively) compared to their non-disadvantaged counterparts (80 per cent and 73 per cent respectively). The level of provision of IT studies and practical skills is significantly higher in schools where Transition Year is provided on an optional basis than in schools with compulsory Transi-tion Year.

Figure 4.3 looks at whether the different subject areas are provided as core areas of knowledge, optional subjects or as both core and op-tional. Academic subjects are generally offered as core subjects or of-fered as both core and optional; in the latter case, all students might study Irish, English and Maths with a choice of four academic subjects from a list of optional subjects, for example. Third-level taster subjects and personal development are more commonly provided as either core or optional as opposed to both core and optional. In general, subjects relat-ing to sports and leisure, IT studies, civic and social studies and work-related learning are more commonly provided as core subjects while cul-tural and skills-based subjects are more commonly provided as optional subjects.

In summary, the main "layers" of Transition Year subjects provided in schools can be identified. In the majority of schools, academic sub-jects, cultural studies, IT studies, sports/leisure, civic/social studies and work-related learning are not only provided but represent compulsory areas of knowledge for Transition Year students.

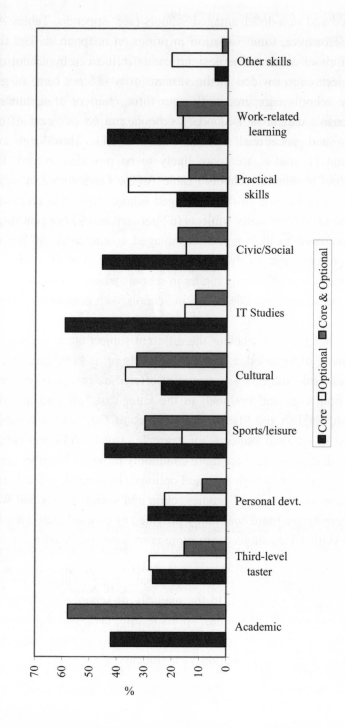

Figure 4.3: The proportion of schools offering the different subject layers as core, optional or both core and optional

Source: Survey of School Principals (2001).

4.4.1 Breadth of programme provision

This section explores the pattern of provision of different subject areas. The number of different subject layers offered by schools surveyed ranges from two to ten. Only a small minority of schools have a narrow Transition Year curriculum, that is, providing four or fewer different subject areas. Around half of schools provide eight or more different subject areas as part of the Transition Year programme (see Figure 4.4).

Figure 4.4: Breadth of programme provision in Transition Year

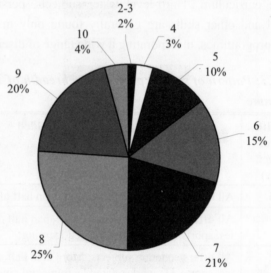

Source: Survey of School Principals (2001).

The number of layers offered was not significantly related to school type, designated disadvantaged status or whether the programme is compulsory or optional. Logistical constraints, however, appear to play an important role as a higher proportion of very small schools offer five or fewer disciplines compared to larger schools and a lower proportion of very small schools offer nine or more disciplines. There was also a significant association between the number of disciplines offered and the nature of subject choice in Transition Year. Over a quarter (28 per cent) of schools which offer subject choice offer their students nine or more disciplines while this was the case for 13 per cent of schools in which core only subjects are offered.

Table 4.3 outlines the pattern of subject provision according to the breadth of the Transition Year programme. All schools, irrespective of the number of disciplines offered, provide academic subjects in Transition Year. Interestingly, there appears to be a hierarchy of subject areas. Where schools provide fewer different disciplines, they tend to focus on academic subjects, cultural studies, sports, IT studies and work-related learning. As the programme becomes more diverse, civic/social studies is incorporated into the curriculum. Third-level taster subjects, personal development, practical and other skills are generally found only in schools providing diverse programmes, incorporating a wide range of disciplines.

Table 4.3: Pattern of subject provision by breadth of Transition Year programme

Breadth (No. of subject areas)	Subjects Provided
2–4	All offer academic subjects. More than half offer cultural studies.
5	All offer academic subjects. More than half offer cultural studies, sports, IT, and work-related learning.
6	All offer academic subjects. More than half offer cultural studies, sports, IT, work-related learning and civic/social studies.
7	All offer academic subjects. More than half offer cultural studies, sports, IT, work-related learning, civic/social studies and third-level taster courses.
8	All offer academic subjects. More than half offer cultural studies, sports, IT, work-related learning, civic/social studies, third-level taster courses and practical skills.
9	All offer academic subjects. More than half offer cultural studies, sports, IT, work-related learning, civic/social studies, third-level taster courses, practical skills and personal development.
10	All offer academic subjects, cultural studies, sports, IT, work-related learning, civic/social studies, third-level taster courses, practical skills, personal development and other skills.

Source: Survey of School Principals (2001).

4.4.2 The provision of academic subjects in Transition Year

Academic subjects are provided as part of the Transition Year programme in all schools. The number of academic subjects provided varies across schools, with an average of nine academic subjects being offered. A greater number of academic subjects are provided than subjects of any other single type, indicating the continued importance of traditional second-level subjects within the Transition Year programme. The number of academic subjects offered does not vary significantly by school type, size or disadvantaged status.

Table 4.4: Proportion of schools providing specified academic subjects within Transition Year

Subject	%	Subject	%
English	100.0	*Science*:	
Maths	98.5	General science	50.2
Irish	97.3	Biology	25.2
		Physics	21.8
History	47.5	Chemistry	20.4
Geography	45.2	Physics-Chemistry	2.1
		Agric. Science	1.2
Languages:			
French	75.1	*Vocational-*	
German	40.7	*technical*:	43.6
Spanish	15.8	Home Economics	14.5
Italian	6.8	Technical Graphics	12.5
Latin	2.5	Construction Studies	9.0
Greek	0.9	Engineering	10.7
		Woodwork	3.4
		Metalwork	11.4
Business:		Technology	
Business Studies	43.3		
Accountancy	8.6		
Economics	6.6	*Arts*:	25.1
Agricultural Econ.	0.3	Art	14.6
		Music	
			3.7
		Classical Studies	

Source: Survey of School Principals (2001).

Table 4.4 indicates the proportion of schools providing the various academic subjects within Transition Year. It is interesting to note that some subjects represent a continuation of the relevant Junior Cert subject (e.g. Science) while others represent the more specialised subject equivalent at Leaving Cert (e.g. Biology, Physics, Chemistry). Irish, English and Maths are provided in almost all schools, irrespective of their school characteristics.[5] French was the next most prevalent subject and the most prevalent European language, being timetabled in three-quarters of all schools. Between 40 and 50 per cent of schools offer Science, History, Geography, Home Economics, Business Studies and/or German, while Art, Biology, Physics and Chemistry are timetabled in a fifth to a quarter of schools. Other subjects are less commonly provided as part of Transition Year, in particular the vocational-technical subjects (with the exception of Home Economics) have relatively low levels of provision.

In sum, there appears to be a number of core academic subjects which are commonly provided as part of the Transition Year programme. These subjects include Irish, English, Maths, French, Science, History, Geography, Home Economics and Business Studies. Although these form the core academic subjects in many schools, there is some variation in provision across different kinds of schools (see Appendix Tables A4.6 to A4.9). History is available in just a third of vocational schools compared with over half of girls' secondary, coed secondary and community/comprehensive schools. However, this pattern is not dissimilar to that found for Junior or Leaving Cert History. Similarly, only 16 per cent of boys' schools provide Home Economics compared with around half of coed secondary schools. Vocational subjects, such as Woodwork and Engineering, are more prevalent in disadvantaged schools while German, Business subjects (such as Accountancy and Economics), Physics and Chemistry were more commonly found in non-disadvantaged schools (Table A4.8). Economics was also significantly more common in larger schools; 11 per cent of very large schools offer Economics while this was the case for just 3 per cent and 6 per cent of medium and small schools respectively (Table A4.7). In addition, History, Geography, German, Spanish and Business Studies are more commonly provided in

---

[5] In the other schools, Irish and/or Maths were integrated into interdisciplinary subjects.

schools that offer a compulsory Transition Year programme. General Science is more common in schools where Transition Year is optional while the more specialised science subjects are more common in schools with a compulsory programme (Table A4.9).

In overall terms, the pattern of variation in academic subject provision across various types of schools resembles the patterns found at Junior and Leaving Cert level, indicating the importance of school tradition and teacher availability (see section 4.2) as factors shaping the content of the Transition Year programme.

4.4.3 Breadth of academic subject provision

The previous section outlined the prevalence of individual academic subjects within the Transition Year programme. In this section, subjects are grouped into subject areas to explore whether particular kinds of academic knowledge are over-represented or under-represented at Transition Year level.

Figure 4.5 illustrates the proportion of schools which offer the various academic knowledge areas. The importance of Irish, English and Maths is clearly evident as all schools offer at least one Irish, English or Maths module. The focus on Irish, English and Maths in Transition Year is understandable for a number of reasons. Firstly, Transition Year guidelines recommend that Irish, English, Maths and one language be timetabled in all Transition Year Programmes. Secondly, interviews with teachers and school management highlighted the importance of providing Irish, English and Maths in order to maintain academic development. Thirdly, teachers and school management view parental support for Transition Year, at least to some degree, as contingent on the continuation of core academic subjects (see Chapter Six).

Figure 4.5: Proportion of Transition Year Programmes offering various academic subject areas

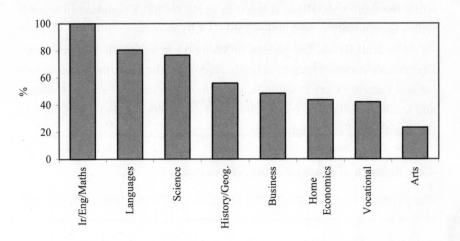

Source: Survey of School Principals (2001).

Another component of Transition Year, languages, is also highly represented in Transition Year programmes as an academic subject. Eighty per cent of schools offer at least one of the following languages: French, German, Spanish, Italian, Latin and Greek. Over three-quarters of schools offer science subjects. While half of schools timetable History and/or Geography, Business and Home Economics are provided in under half of the schools surveyed. While individual vocational subjects appeared under-represented within Transition Year (see Table 4.4), it should be noted that forty per cent of schools offer at least one vocational/technological subject.[6] Fewer than a quarter of schools provide Art and/or Music as academic subjects to Transition Year students.

The provision of many academic subject areas, in particular, Vocational, Home Economics, Business and, to a lesser extent, History/Geography subjects, differs significantly by school type (see Table 4.5). In relation to business subjects, the highest timetabled provision is found in secondary schools (53–59 per cent) with significantly lower levels of provision in vocational schools (31 per cent). Home Economics is more

---

[6] Vocational subjects being Technical Graphics, Metalwork, Woodwork, Construction Studies, Engineering, and Technology.

prevalent in girls' secondary schools with particularly low levels of provision in boys' schools. A similar pattern was evident in relation to arts
subjects (Art and Music). In relation to vocational subjects, almost two-
thirds of vocational and community/comprehensive schools offer these
subjects in Transition Year compared with a minority of secondary, especially girls', schools.

*Table 4.5: The proportion of schools timetabling various academic
knowledge areas*

	Voca-tional	History/ Geog.	Busi-ness	H.E	Art/ Music	Science	Lang
Boys' Sec.	35.0	55.7	59.0	16.4	13.3	76.7	78.3
Girls' Sec.	19.2	56.6	52.5	60.0	43.4	78.8	82.8
Coed Sec.	42.6	63.9	52.5	49.2	27.9	82.0	72.6
Vocational	64.3	42.0	31.4	42.0	28.6	67.1	82.9
Comm./Comp.	65.9	65.9	44.2	38.6	36.4	81.8	86.0
Significance	*p<.001*	*p<.10*	*p<.05*	*p<.001*	*p<.01*	*NS*	*NS*

Source: Survey of School Principals (2001).

There is no significant association between types of academic subject
areas provided and school size (see Appendix Table A4.10). However,
vocational subjects are more prevalent in designated disadvantaged
schools, being offered in 56 per cent of such schools compared with 37
per cent of their non-disadvantaged counterparts (Table A4.11).

In summary, Irish, English, Maths, Languages, Sciences and History/
Geography are well represented in Transition Year programmes. Business, Home Economics and vocational subjects are represented in a large
minority of Transition Year programmes. In overall terms, the provision
of academic subjects tends to reflect the school ethos and tradition within
particular school sectors; in other words, the kinds of academic subjects
provided within Transition Year tend to be a subset of those provided by
a school at Junior and Leaving Cert levels.

4.4.4 Time allocated to different subjects

The previous section has indicated the prevalence of academic subjects within the Transition Year curriculum. Interviews conducted with subject teachers in the case-study schools allowed us to explore the amount of time allocated to the different types of subjects, both academic and non-academic. Information was collected from 142 subject teachers regarding the number of class periods per week based on their main subject taught to Transition Year students. Subjects are grouped into two categories; "traditional" academic subjects and more "innovative" Transition Year subjects. On average, more class periods are allocated to academic subjects than to "innovative" subjects within the case-study schools (see Table 4.6).

Table 4.6: Number of class periods by subject type within Transition Year

	Average per week	N
Academic subjects	4.13	83
Innovative Transition Year subjects	3.73	45

Source: Case-studies of schools.

The information on number of class periods can be broken down further across the different knowledge areas (see Table 4.7). The vast majority of teachers teaching academic subjects are allocated four or more class periods per week. IT studies, third-level taster subjects and sports/leisure are usually allocated four or more periods per week. In contrast, personal development and civic/social studies are most commonly allocated three periods per week.

Table 4.8 indicates the importance of Irish, English and Maths, with 93 per cent of Irish, English or Maths teachers being allocated four or more weekly periods of these subjects per week. This pattern was evident across all case-study schools. Most other academic subjects were allocated four or more weekly periods in all of the case-study schools. The exceptions are Science subjects and arts subjects, which are sometimes allocated only two or three periods per week.

Table 4.7: Number of class periods by knowledge area (%)

	Two	Three	Four or more
Academic	6.3	7.6	86.1
Third-level taster	12.5	18.8	68.8
Personal development	20.0	60.0	20.0
Sports/leisure	12.5	25.0	62.5
IT studies	20.0	10.0	70.0
Civic/social studies	0.0	63.6	36.4
Practical skills	12.5	37.5	50.0
Other skills	66.7	33.3	0.0

Source: Case-studies of schools.

Table 4.8: Number of class periods by academic subject (case-study schools) (%)

	Two	Three	Four or more
Irish/English/Maths	2.4	4.8	92.9
Languages	9.1	0.0	90.9
Sciences	12.5	25.0	62.5
Vocational subjects	0.0	0.0	100.0
Business subjects	0.0	0.0	100.0
Home Economics	0.0	0.0	100.0
Arts	20.0	20.0	60.0

Source: Case-studies of schools.

In sum, there appears to be a core set of subject areas which are generally incorporated into the Transition Year programme; these include academic subjects, cultural studies, sports, IT studies, civic/social studies and work-related learning. The type of academic subjects provided tends to reflect school ethos and teacher availability. An average of nine "traditional" academic subjects are provided within Transition Year and academic subjects tend to be allocated somewhat more time within the programme.

4.5 WORK EXPERIENCE IN TRANSITION YEAR

This section examines the place of work experience within the Transition Year programme. Transition Year students can engage in two types of work: work experience placement(s) as an essential prerequisite of the Transition Year programme and paid part-time employment. While the marked growth in the incorporation of work experience into second-level education can be seen as part of a wider attempt to integrate education and work, an increase in the prevalence of part-time work among students can be seen as a consequence of the economic boom with more and more teenagers looking to part-time work as a means of subsidising their incomes (see McCoy, Smyth, forthcoming). The prevalence of part-time work among Transition Year students is documented and discussed in Chapter Eight while this section focuses on formal work experience placements within Transition Year.

According to the Department of Education guidelines:

> It is intended that the Transition Year should create opportunities to vary the learning environment and to dispel the notion that learning is something that happens only, or even most effectively, within the classroom. One of the ways of doing this, and of providing an orientation towards the world of work, is to include a component of actual work experience.

Work-related learning in preparation for adult working life is an important component of the Transition Year mission in providing a basis for personal development, preparation for adult life and maturity. Nonetheless, despite the widespread use of this approach to learning in Transition Year, very little systematic research has been undertaken to justify the premise on which work experience is based (McKenna and O'Maolmhuire, 2000). An evaluation study by Egan and O'Reilly (1997) found that teachers felt that all students would benefit from work experience. A number of additional studies have touched on the work-related learning undertaken by Transition Year students, with many highlighting the ambiguous nature of work experience in Transition Year (Department of Education, 1996; McKenna and O'Maolmhuire, 2000). The Inspectorate Report stated that "most schools saw work experience as a vital element in TY, providing pupils with alternative learning environments, acquainting them with the world of work and offering positive opportunities for personal growth and development" (1996, p. 2). However, the emphasis on, and nature of, work experience provided was seen as related to the different traditions of the school and the varied socio-economic backgrounds of the students. Information from the postal survey of principals, supplemented with in-depth accounts from the case-study schools, allowed us to explore the prevalence and nature of formal work experience within the Transition Year programme.

4.5.1 Prevalence of work experience

The postal survey reveals that the majority (97 per cent) of schools offer all of their Transition Year students work experience, with a very small number of schools providing work experience for only some students or none at all. Reasons for not offering all students work experience included a lack of available places for student employees, students' choosing not to participate in work experience or students being precluded from participating because of behavioural problems. Unfortunately, the smaller proportion of schools who do not offer any work experience for their students offered no explanations as to why this may be the case. However, previous research has indicated that in some cases students were perceived as being too young to derive any significant benefits from such an experience, while other schools did not consider work experience sufficiently important or cited financial constraints as a result of insurance difficulties (McKenna and O'Maolmhuire, 2000). The majority of schools surveyed for this study offer work experience irrespective of school type, size or region. However, work experience is somewhat more likely to be provided for all students in schools where Transition Year is optional rather than compulsory (98 per cent compared with 95 per cent).

In general, students spend an average of fifteen days on work experience, with all schools offering a minimum of five days (or one working week's) experience. Students in boys' secondary schools spend somewhat more, and those in girls' and community/comprehensive schools somewhat less, time on work experience. Students who attend schools where Transition Year is optional tend to spend slightly more days on work experience than those in schools where the programme is compulsory, although the difference is not statistically significant. This may reflect some difficulties in finding suitable placements and providing adequate preparation where a larger cohort of students is involved. While the Inspectorate Report (1996) indicated that more vocationally oriented schools had longer work experience placements than more "academic" schools, no such pattern was evident from our study. Variation in the length of work experience placement was apparent among the case-study schools with students in Willis St. and Manners Mall spending four weeks in total on work experience compared to two weeks in most of the other case-study schools.

As well as differing in the length of time spent on work placement, schools were found to vary in how they organise the work experience period. For example, students in Victoria St. work for a block of two weeks while students in Willis St. work for two separate two-week periods. In contrast, students attending Hopper St. work one day a week for one term. The latter approach was seen as potentially more disruptive by staff in the school.

4.5.2 Organisation of work experience in Transition Year

Schools adopt different approaches to the organisation of work experience placements within Transition Year. Among the case-study schools, most prefer students to locate their own work placements. In general, students were encouraged to arrange their own work placement in order to experience job search and coping with the world of work:

> It was the school's expectation that they would be proactive themselves or their parents might help them to find work placements. I'd say most of them did (Guidance Counsellor, Hopper St.).

In Willis St., where students have two two-week blocs of work placement, students are expected to find their own placement for the first bloc and then are given guidance in finding the second placement.

However, some students were seen to need more help than others in obtaining employment, at which point school personnel tended to intervene:

> With a few of them I had to work a little bit harder to organise placements but in that it came to the point that a few of them just didn't have placements or hadn't done very much about it. I had to sit them down. I had to make telephone calls and I was able to work from a list of placements from last year and it worked out well (Guidance Counsellor, Hopper St.).

Some teachers felt that it was difficult to motivate students to participate in work experience due to their prior part-time job commitments. This feeling was particularly evident in Cuba and Hopper St., schools with more working-class student intakes:

> There's difficulties getting places but it's more from the end of trying to get the students interested. It's all about creating student interest because if they are working in part-time jobs they think "fine, I'll just continue on with my part-time job". . . so it's beating on their heads and it's building the enthusiasm (Principal, Cuba St.).

> I suppose what we would have difficulty with is persuading parents that there is a difference between work and a part-time job and doing work experience and the different focus and there would also be an issue with some parents about them leaving the local community (Principal, Hopper St.).

While problems of motivating students were also reported in another working-class school, Manners Mall, students were encouraged to use the placement to explore different kinds of work than they had already been exposed to:

> We push them very hard to get placements which are in areas that they wouldn't have experience of, and they tend to go back to the shops and the places they have part-time work. That would be one of our biggest difficulties. But a good lot of them will go and get experience in places other than that. Our aim is to get them to go to places other than the shops, or the hairdressers, or wherever they might have part-time jobs (Principal, Manners Mall).

Each of the case-study schools drew on an active network of teachers, Transition Year co-ordinators and/or guidance counsellors to aid in organising work placements. According to the TYCSS study (2001), the second most important task of a Transition Year Co-ordinator is the organisation of work experience and this was also evident in our case-study schools. In addition, it appears that guidance counsellors also play a vital role in the allocation and organisation of work placements. In the spirit of Transition Year, the organisation of work experience in the majority of schools involves partnerships and interaction between teachers, students, past pupils, local companies and businesses as well as parents:

> We use the contacts of the former students of the school. We have loads of contacts after a number of years so I have a fair few contacts myself that I have built up. Between everything and between staff contacts and links, we place people anywhere and everywhere (Guidance Counsellor, Mt. Cook).

> [How they obtain work experience] varies widely. They get work in companies maybe that their parents know or we have a core group of employers that one of the teachers can ask for work experience for the students in the school (TY Co-ordinator, Hopper St).

However, in a number of schools the main responsibility lies with the Transition Year Co-ordinator. This was evident in Cuba St., where the organisation of work placements was contingent on the co-ordinator's willingness to take on the task:

> Actually for the first few years of the programme we didn't have work experience because we didn't have someone who was willing and able to take the responsibility . . . until the TYC came along (Principal, Cuba St.).

Overall, students in the case-study schools were encouraged to obtain their own placements as part of the learning process. However, in many instances, school staff, especially the Transition Year co-ordinator and guidance counsellor, were involved in helping students to find placements, especially those students who were less motivated about the process.

4.5.3 Preparation for work experience

In preparation for work experience, a number of methods such as questionnaires, videos, enterprise classes and checklists are used to prepare and brief students for their work placements. Group interviews with students explored how well prepared students felt prior to their placement.

A number of students outlined that they felt well prepared for the task in hand given the classes that they had attended during the course of Transition Year:

> I had to make loads of phone calls and write away and everything. But I think it was easier for people who had done personal development because that's all about CVs and writing away, interviews and things like that. I had done it before so it was easier then (Student, Mt. Cook).

> Yes, we had enterprise class. They told us what to do, how to behave. A guy came over and told us stuff and gave us a sheet handout to plan out our time (Student, Cuba St).

While this pattern was evident in most of the schools, a number of students outlined that they would have appreciated more input from teachers regarding work experience:

> A careers teacher talked to us a bit about it. There wasn't really anything telling you how to act. They just said the basic things, just to be punctual, to be mannerly. You know yourself — they really left it up to us (Student, Victoria St).

> We were chucked in at the deep end (Student, Mt. Cook).

In addition, some students, particularly those who had worked before, felt that such preparation was not necessary:

> Probably most of us have experience, we have all worked before, part-time or whatever (Student, Hopper St).

> Most of us would know from experience . . . how to act. We wouldn't be running around like raving lunatics (Student, Victoria St).

> Interviewer: And before you went out on your experience, did you have a class or anything that explained what you should be doing?

> Student: No, nothing, but you don't really need one (Student, Manners Mall).

Even within a school, variation in preparation and briefing practices between Transition Year classes was evident, with some Transition Year classes receiving more preparation than others:

> First student: Well our class got a checklist of things to do before you start your job.
>
> Second student: We didn't get that (Wallace St.).

In sum, variation was evident between and within schools in the amount of preparation that was provided for students taking part in work experience. The following section explores the nature of those placements.

4.5.4 The nature of work experience

> It varies from working in Superquinn to working in RTÉ to working in England. We have had the odd person go to England. A lot of them would work in schools as assistants to the teachers but there are all kinds of jobs, the Garda station, the fire station, county council. Some of them would work in building sites and all sorts of things (Guidance Counsellor, Willis St.).

The interviews conducted with Transition Year co-ordinators, principals and guidance counsellors highlighted the range of different work experience placements participated in by students. In general, two main types of work placements were evident among students in the case-study schools. Firstly, there are placements that can be deemed "career sampling" where students get to try out jobs they might be interested in working at in the future. In such cases, the work experience is seen as an opportunity for students to think about their future aspirations, give them a taste of responsibility and experience as well as encourage socialisation, maturity and work interaction with adults. Secondly, there are work placements which are not career sampling but resemble part-time jobs. This involves students obtaining work experience from their usual part-time job or even choosing placements in which they were likely to be "kept on" as paid part-time workers. Concern was expressed by a number of school staff regarding the quality of such work experience placements.

Irrespective of the nature of the job undertaken, whether a "career" or "part-time job", it was evident from the group interviews with students that they generally participate in work that they themselves are interested in. More importantly, students appear to learn from their experience in the work place. For example, one student in Willis St. aspired to become an electrician and had obtained work experience in an electrical shop. He felt that the experience of learning about the tasks of an electrician helped to clarify his decision in pursuing this trade. Another student in this school had always wanted to be a primary school teacher, but after the placement, felt that it was not satisfactory and did not intend to pursue it as a career option. A similar experience was reported by another student:

> It's good because now I know what I want to do when I leave. I did two weeks' work experience in hairdressing and I thought I would really like it. But what I would really like is just to do my own hair. But somebody else's, I didn't like it as much as I thought I would (Student, Victoria St.).

Additionally, work experience in Transition Year was seen as helping senior cycle students clarify the distinction between part-time jobs and career jobs:

> It was different because your part-time job is just — you know you have to do it — but the work experience is much different. I only worked in a food restaurant but it was much different. It was better than the part-time job. The work in the school is better (Student, Cuba St.).

In sum, students tended to take different approaches to their work experience placement, with some students using the placement to try a job they were interested in pursuing while other students tended to take jobs which resembled their paid part-time jobs. The group who engaged in "career sampling" saw the placement as helping to inform their long-term career choices.

4.5.5 Follow-up and assessment

It has been recommended that for a work placement to be a worthwhile learning experience, students need not only to be well briefed beforehand but also debriefed afterwards (McKenna and O'Maolmhuire, 2000).

Among the case-study schools, it was evident that a number of schools take part in on-site visits to their Transition Year students during their placements. This was common practice among Transition Year co-ordinators in Willis St., Manners Mall, Mt. Cook, and Victoria St. schools:

> The TYC visits the workplace if it is local and otherwise phones the employer at least once during the visit (TY Co-ordinator, Manners Mall).

> We call out to each individual student during the course of their work experience if they are within distance from the school (TY Co-ordinator, Willis St.).

In other cases, direct contact was made with the employer:

> The co-ordinator would maybe ring or call if it's convenient but ringing is probably easier (Principal, Victoria St.).

In addition, a number of schools asked employers to complete an assessment form on the student with this information supplemented by self-assessment on the part of the student:

> We get in touch with the employer and send them out an assessment form to be filled out on the student. Then we get the students to fill out an assessment form themselves and how they felt they got on. . . . At the end of the year, the student is interviewed and given details of the assessment that the employer gave them and we'll look at what he thought and how he got on during the work experience and show them the two sets of the two periods of work experience. So again there's a lot of time taken up getting after that number of students (TY Co-ordinator, Willis St.).

> Students are evaluated by their employer and they would also evaluate it from their own point of view what they felt they got from the experience and so on. It's good to have that happening (TY Co-ordinator, Mt. Cook).

As with preparation for work experience, the extent of direct contact with employers and follow-up work with students varied across the case-study schools.

4.5.6 Perceived effectiveness of work experience

In general, the majority of key personnel interviewed felt that work experience in Transition Year was a positive experience for students. The benefits listed included more informed subject choice for Leaving Certificate and third-level education along with an increased awareness of possible careers:

> If they focus on a career area that they want to explore, it [the work experience] will give them an insight into that and a number of them will go to [the local university], they will go to the IT, they will get into accounting firms and they will really focus on a career area (Guidance Counsellor, Victoria St.).

> There's no doubt that many students have gained quite a bit from the work experience, some either to dismiss what they have done and say "I always wanted to be a such and such. I have tried it out and it's terrible". If nothing else they learn about the real work place and even though it's quite a short time, many of them would gain (Guidance Counsellor, Willis St).

But in another school this was not the feeling:

> It's very fluid now the whole career thing and some of the students don't want the settled existence that I was brought up with in the 60s, 70s. The whole attitude is different and, of course, there is more resources out there, financial and otherwise, so I don't think it has a major influence, some cases it will but in a lot of cases it won't (Guidance Counsellor, Mt. Cook).

In sum, while almost all schools provide work experience as part of the Transition Year programme, there is variation across schools in the length of the placement, the degree of active involvement of students in obtaining placements, and extent of preparation for, and follow-up of, the placement itself.

4.6 THE PROVISION OF CAREER GUIDANCE IN TRANSITION YEAR

One of the central aims of Transition Year is to provide education through experience of adult working life as a basis for personal development and maturity. While work experience placements are an obvious way of addressing this objective, they must be seen within the broader context of career guidance and information within Transition Year. Among the case-study schools, variation is evident in the extent to which Transition Year students have timetabled or other organised sessions of career guidance. While students in Cuba St. and Willis St. schools have timetabled classes, in the other case-study schools students often have only one or two formal sessions with a guidance counsellor.

The absence of timetabled sessions with Transition Year students was often attributed to the fact that priority is given to providing guidance time to Junior Certificate and senior cycle classes:

> I would obviously give priority to sixth and fifth years. And then later on in the year I would look at third years (Guidance Counsellor, Mount Cook).

> A lot of my timetabled work would be with sixth years and fifth years. . . . I would also have a fair input to third year students (Guidance Counsellor, Wallace St.).

> I have very little involvement with TY and I have to say I feel guilty about it (Guidance Counsellor, Wallace St.).

The lack of timetabled classes was often due to logistical constraints, particularly lack of time and resources, rather than deliberate policy. This was particularly evident in Hopper St., Wallace St. and Victoria St. schools:

> I have just very limited timetabled classes [with any students]. I think I just have three class periods in the week (Guidance Counsellor, Hopper St.).

> At the start there was a guidance module, a ten week module, but for some reason it went from the Transition Year timetable and I feel dreadfully guilty because I actually don't get to see them and I must say they tend to come down my list a bit because it's just pressure of work really (Guidance Counsellor, Wallace St.).

> There have been years when I was timetabled for Transition Year but I haven't been timetabled this year for Transition Year (Guidance Counsellor, Victoria St.).

In Mount Cook, the absence of timetabled classes for Transition Year students was seen as related to a lack of time, in the context of the approach taken to guidance counselling:

> There are no timetabled classes in fourth year, because it makes it difficult in terms of trying to get around individually to all the students in the school. I'm a firm believer that guidance counselling is about . . . seeing people individually and dealing with them individually. You can't deal with them collectively. In the class situation we can't do it, if you want to motivate them, it's got to be individual (Guidance Counsellor, Mount Cook).

However, many career guidance teachers emphasised that Transition Year students had received timetabled guidance at Junior Certificate level and this was often represented as an alternative to providing time-tabled classes in Transition Year. It was often felt that the work experience module and experience of additional subject choice in Transition Year contributed to career guidance in a more general sense:

> The actual Transition Year experience itself is good for them and the exposure they get to the various subjects, it gives them a fairly good grounding. . . . By fifth year, most of them are in fact quite focused and have a fair idea what they want. They are just looking for maybe fine detail on choices (Guidance Counsellor, Wallace St.).

> They [TY students] pick their [LC] subjects after Easter. Now a lot of those would have some idea of the subjects they are choosing because they would have gone through this again in third year. Having said that a lot of them would have their minds made up doing Transition Year in third year anyway and probably would just focus on that rather than the subjects for fifth year (Guidance Counsellor, Victoria St.).

Students in Hopper St., Victoria St. and Mount Cook are allocated one or two informal sessions throughout the year with a guidance teacher. These classes generally focus on work experience preparation or subject choice for Leaving Certificate:

> I do take them for their subject choice options. We would have organised the trips to college careers days and that type of thing (Guidance Counsellor, Victoria St.).

> In the Summer term, I see fourth year students and I talk to them as a group. We do aptitude tests (not that I put a lot of emphasis into that to be honest with you). We play around with a whole lot of things to try and get them started in the real world as distinct from the academic world, we take it from there and we build on that in fifth year (Guidance Counsellor, Mount Cook).

> The principal asked me at the start of the year to assist the Transition Year Co-ordinator in organising work placements for one of the Transition Year classes (Guidance Counsellor, Hopper St.).

Cuba St. and Willis St. were the only case-study schools with a structured career guidance programme, where classes are timetabled for Transition Year students. In both of these schools, the provision of career guidance to Transition Year students was seen to be of major importance with a lot of emphasis placed on career orientation. For this, students are allocated an hour a week for the whole year:

> I do two main areas; one is careers-based and the other is etiquette. I give students information and I guide them towards accessing the information themselves (Guidance Counsellor, Willis St.).

> Transition Year, it's probably one of the most important years. I really encourage them to take something that they like the idea of as opposed to something that they think they can realistically get. So a lot of it is about aspiration building (Guidance Counsellor, Cuba St.).

Perhaps the most impressive feature of these programmes was the requirement that each student completes an in-depth careers research project. This project is intended to promote some of the key objectives of the Transition Year programme, including interdisciplinary learning, aspiration building, and self-directed learning while also focusing on the development of research and presentation skills. Because students have to present their work upon completion of the project, all students are fully informed about the academic requirements (including subjects, levels and points needed at Leaving Certificate) as well as the social and other skills needed for a particular profession.

Given that student attitudes at junior cycle level are found to be predictive of later decisions regarding educational participation (Smyth and Hannan, 2002), perhaps the most innovative aspect of this type of careers teaching is that students are given direction earlier on in senior cycle. The benefits of providing in-depth career guidance in Transition Year were outlined by both teachers involved:

> I don't have fifth years so by the time they get to sixth year, if they don't know the prospectuses and if they can't find their way through the prospectus it's going to be too late in sixth year by the time they find out. It's going to be CAO time and so forth (Guidance Counsellor, Willis St.).

> So literally, when I come to fifth year and sixth year I have no work to do with them in that area. This is because they have done it all in fourth year. They know the process and, when they have actually worked through a process in a real sense, the product is very easily managed (Guidance Counsellor, Cuba St.).

In sum, variation was evident among the case-study schools in the role of career guidance within the Transition Year programme. The lack of guidance time allocated to Transition Year students tended to reflect overall resource constraints. In two schools, the presence of structured guidance programmes within Transition Year was seen as providing useful preparation for making later career choices as well as facilitating the development of independent learning and research skills.

4.7 CONCLUSIONS

The majority of schools use Transition Year as an opportunity for students to sample subjects with the choice of Leaving Certificate subjects taking place late in the year. However, schools differ in the extent of choice within Transition Year, with a significant minority of schools requiring all students to take the same subjects.

Schools differ in the content of the Transition Year programme, although the nucleus of the programme encompasses academic, cultural, sports, computing, work-related learning and civic/social subjects. Logistical constraints appear to play a role in shaping programme content with very small schools being less likely to offer diverse programmes.

Academic subjects represent an important core of the Transition Year programme with students taking a significant number of academic subjects and those subjects taking up more time than other subjects. The pattern of academic subject provision within Transition Year tends to reflect the overall school ethos and tradition, indicating the role of teacher availability in shaping the content of the programme. Irish, English, Maths, Languages and Science subjects are provided within the vast majority of Transition Year programmes with greater variation between schools in exposure to History/Geography, Business, Home Economics, vocational and arts subjects.

Almost all schools provide work experience for all of their students. However, the nature of work experience varies in duration and quality with some students taking placements which closely resemble part-time jobs rather than using the experience to engage in "career sampling". The provision of formal career guidance for Transition Year students varies across schools with regular sessions provided for students in only two of the case-study schools.

APPENDIX TABLES

Appendix Table A4.1: Proportion of schools offering subject areas by school type

Discipline	Boys' Sec.	Girls' Sec.	Coed Sec.	Voca-tional	Comm. /Comp.	Signif.
Academic subjects	100.0	100.0	100.0	100.0	100.0	NS
Culture	85.2	94.9	95.1	88.6	97.7	$p<.10$
Sports & Leisure	81.7	88.9	86.9	90.0	88.4	NS
IT Studies	86.7	87.9	77.0	88.6	95.3	$p<.10$
Civic/Social	75.4	87.9	67.7	68.6	76.7	$p<.05$
Work-related learning	73.3	73.7	80.3	78.3	81.8	NS
Third-level taster	68.3	67.7	62.9	70.0	68.2	NS
Practical skills	59.0	63.0	68.9	61.4	50.0	NS
Personal dev.	45.9	63.0	54.1	65.2	63.6	NS
Other skills	19.7	26.3	24.2	26.1	9.1	NS
N	*63*	*105*	*63*	*64*	*39*	

Note: NS — not statistically significant.

Source: Survey of School Principals (2001).

Table A4.2: Proportion of schools offering the various disciplines by school size

Discipline	<400	400–599	600+	Significance
Academic subjects	100.0	100.0	100.0	NS
Culture	90.9	91.3	94.6	NS
Sports & Leisure	86.7	87.4	86.6	NS
IT Studies	86.0	81.6	91.9	p<.10
Civic/Social	74.2	81.6	74.8	NS
Work-related learning	76.7	75.7	78.4	NS
Third-level taster	60.0	68.9	74.1	p<.10
Practical skills	65.0	58.3	60.4	NS
Personal development	55.0	57.3	64.9	NS
Other skills	24.2	24.3	18.9	NS
N	*122*	*108*	*104*	

Note: NS — not statistically significant.

Source: Survey of School Principals (2001).

Table A4.3: Proportion of schools offering subject disciplines by disadvantaged status

Discipline	Disadvantaged	Not Disadvan.	Significance
Academic subjects	100.0	100.0	NS
Culture	93.2	91.9	NS
Sports & Leisure	92.0	85.4	p<.10
IT Studies	87.4	86.2	NS
Civic/Social	66.7	80.2	p<.01
Work-related learning	73.9	77.7	NS
Third-level taster	52.9	72.9	p<.001
Practical skills	36.4	39.3	NS
Personal development	67.8	55.9	p<.05
Other skills	17.2	24.0	NS
N	*84*	*250*	

Note: NS — not statistically significant.

Source: Survey of School Principals (2001).

Table A4.4: Proportion of schools offering subject disciplines by nature of Transition Year provision

Discipline	Compulsory	Optional	Significance
Academic subjects	100.0	100.0	NS
Culture	92.5	92.1	NS
Sports & Leisure	89.9	86.2	NS
IT Studies	80.0	88.6	p<.05
Civic/Social	77.5	76.4	NS
Work-related learning	74.7	78.0	NS
Third-level taster	69.6	66.9	NS
Practical skills	23.8	43.7	p<.001
Personal development	62.5	57.5	NS
Other skills	25.3	21.3	NS
N	80	253	

Note: NS — not statistically significant.

Source: Survey of School Principals (2001).

Table A4.5: Provision of subject areas by breadth of programme provision (number of disciplines timetabled)

	2-3	4	5	6	7	8	9	10
Academic	100	100	100	100	100	100	100	100
Cultural studies	60.0	60.0	73.5	92.0	92.9	98.0	98.5	100
Sports/Leisure	40.0	50.0	73.5	70.0	90.0	94.3	98.5	100
IT Studies		50.0	61.8	90.0	88.6	88.6	98.5	100
Work-related learning		30.0	52.9	60.0	71.4	86.2	100	100
Civic/Social studies	20.0	40.0	44.1	68.0	67.1	92.0	95.5	100
Third-level taster	40.0	20.0	35.3	40.0	68.6	78.2	92.4	100
Practical Skills	20.0	20.0	26.5	48.0	52.9	71.3	84.8	100
Personal Development		30.0	35.3	28.0	57.1	64.4	87.9	100
Other Skills				4.0	11.4	26.4	43.9	100
No. of schools	5	10	34	50	70	86	66	14

Source: Survey of School Principals (2001).

Table A4.6: Proportion of schools offering various academic subjects by school type (Subjects provided by more than 10 schools only)

	Boys' Sec.	Girls' Sec.	Coed Sec.	Voca-tional	Comm./ Comp.	Signif.
English	100.0	100.0	100.0	100.0	100.0	NS
Irish	98.3	100.0	96.7	92.9	97.7	p<.10
Maths	98.3	98.0	98.4	100.0	97.7	NS
History	47.5	53.0	54.1	32.9	50.0	p<.10
Geography	50.8	46.0	54.8	31.4	44.2	p<.10
French	75.0	77.0	68.9	80.0	72.7	NS
German	43.5	50.5	39.3	28.6	36.4	p<.10
Spanish	14.8	19.2	19.7	8.7	15.9	NS
Italian	8.3	9.1	6.6	1.4	6.8	NS
Business Studies	50.8	46.0	50.8	28.6	38.6	p<.05
Accountancy	13.0	11.0	6.6	4.3	6.8	NS
Economics	14.8	4.0	8.2	0.0	9.3	p<.01
Science	41.7	51.0	62.3	44.3	54.5	NS
Biology	31.7	26.3	16.4	24.3	27.3	NS
Physics	36.7	19.2	18.0	18.6	18.6	p<.10
Chemistry	30.0	23.0	18.0	13.0	15.9	NS
Home Economics	16.4	60.0	49.2	42.0	38.6	p<.001
Technical Graphics	18.0	5.0	9.8	24.3	23.3	p<.01
Construction Studies	14.8	0.0	11.5	20.0	27.3	p<.001
Engineering	1.6	1.0	1.6	21.4	27.9	p<.001
Woodwork	1.7	4.0	18.0	18.8	15.9	p<.001
Metalwork	3.3	0.0	3.3	8.7	2.3	p<.05
Technology	9.8	12.0	9.8	10.0	18.2	NS
Art	8.3	36.0	24.6	22.9	27.3	p<.01
Music	6.6	23.2	9.8	11.4	18.2	p<.05
Classical Studies	4.9	6.0	3.3	0.0	4.5	NS

Note: NS — not statistically significant.

Source: Survey of School Principals (2001).

Table A4.7: Proportion of schools offering various academic subjects by school size (Subjects offered by more than 10 schools only)

	<400	400–599	>600	Significance
English	100.0	100.0	100.0	NS
Irish	96.7	99.0	96.2	NS
Maths	99.2	100.0	96.4	p<.10
History	49.2	47.6	45.5	NS
Geography	50.8	44.7	39.6	NS
French	74.2	79.6	72.1	NS
German	35.5	40.8	46.8	NS
Spanish	12.5	13.6	21.6	NS
Italian	4.2	5.8	10.7	NS
Business Studies	46.3	40.8	42.3	NS
Accountancy	10.8	5.8	9.0	NS
Economics	5.8	2.9	10.8	p<.10
Science	45.0	47.6	57.7	NS
Biology	28.1	27.2	19.8	NS
Physics	25.0	22.3	18.0	NS
Chemistry	20.0	20.4	20.7	NS
Home Economics	40.8	43.7	45.9	NS
Technical Graphics	14.0	12.6	16.2	NS
Construction Studies	15.8	12.6	9.0	NS
Engineering	6.7	9.7	10.8	NS
Woodwork	10.7	9.7	11.7	NS
Metalwork	5.8	1.9	1.8	NS
Technology	10.0	9.7	14.4	NS
Art	25.0	31.1	19.8	NS
Music	10.7	19.4	15.3	NS
Classical Studies	3.3	3.9	3.6	NS

Note: NS — not statistically significant.

Source: Survey of School Principals (2001).

Table A4.8: Proportion of schools offering various academic subjects by disadvantaged status (Subjects offered by more than 10 schools only)

	Disadvantaged	Not Disadvantaged	Significance
English	100.0	100.0	NS
Irish	96.6	97.6	NS
Maths	98.9	98.4	NS
History	46.6	47.8	NS
Geography	46.6	44.7	NS
French	73.9	75.3	NS
German	34.1	43.1	$p<.10$
Spanish	11.5	17.0	NS
Italian	5.7	7.3	NS
Business Studies	42.5	43.5	NS
Accountancy	3.4	10.5	$p<.05$
Economics	0.0	8.9	$p<.001$
Science	54.5	48.6	NS
Biology	21.8	26.3	NS
Physics	16.1	23.9	$p<.10$
Chemistry	14.8	22.7	$p<.10$
Home Economics	46.0	42.7	NS
Technical Graphics	15.9	14.2	NS
Construction Studies	18.2	10.5	$p<.10$
Engineering	14.8	6.9	$p<.05$
Woodwork	20.7	7.3	$p<.001$
Metalwork	4.5	3.2	NS
Technology	10.3	11.7	NS
Art	27.3	24.3	NS
Music	18.2	13.4	NS
Classical Studies	2.3	4.5	NS

Note: NS — not statistically significant.

Source: Survey of School Principals (2001).

Table A4.9: Proportion of schools offering various academic subjects by nature of Transition Year provision (Subjects offered by more than 10 schools only)

	Compulsory	Optional	Significance
English	100.0	100.0	NS
Irish	100.0	96.9	NS
Maths	100.0	98.0	NS
History	65.0	42.1	p<.001
Geography	58.2	41.3	p<.01
French	78.5	74.4	NS
German	51.3	37.4	p<.05
Spanish	25.0	13.0	p<.05
Italian	8.9	6.3	NS
Business Studies	54.4	39.5	p<.05
Accountancy	20.3	4.7	p<.001
Economics	13.8	4.3	p<.01
Science	27.8	57.5	p<.001
Biology	51.3	16.9	p<.001
Physics	45.0	15.0	p<.001
Chemistry	40.5	14.2	p<.001
Home Economics	40.5	44.1	NS
Technical Graphics	25.3	11.0	p<.01
Construction Studies	19.0	10.2	p<.05
Engineering	17.7	6.3	p<.01
Woodwork	8.9	11.4	NS
Metalwork	3.8	3.1	NS
Technology	11.4	11.4	NS
Art	29.1	23.6	NS
Music	16.3	14.2	NS
Classical Studies	7.5	2.8	p<.10

Note: NS — not statistically significant.

Source: Survey of School Principals (2001).

Table A4.10: Proportion of schools offering academic subject areas by school size

Academic Subject Area	<400	400–599	>600	Signif.
Irish, English, Maths	100.0	100.0	100.0	NS
Languages	78.3	84.5	79.3	NS
Science	77.5	74.8	78.4	NS
History/Geography	60.0	56.3	51.4	NS
Home Economics	40.8	43.7	45.9	NS
Business	50.8	42.7	50.5	NS
Vocational	44.2	36.9	44.1	NS
Art/Music	29.8	35.9	29.7	NS

Table A4.11: Proportion of schools offering academic subjects areas by disadvantaged status

Academic Subject Area	Disadvantaged	Not Disadvantaged	Significance
Irish, English, Maths	100.0	100.0	NS
Languages	81.8	80.1	NS
Science	78.4	76.1	NS
History/Geography	57.5	55.5	NS
Home Economics	46.0	42.7	NS
Business	42.5	50.2	NS
Vocational	56.3	36.8	p<.001
Art/Music	36.8	29.6	NS

Chapter Five

MANAGEMENT AND ORGANISATION OF TRANSITION YEAR IN PRACTICE

INTRODUCTION

Chapter Four has outlined the content of Transition Year programmes in different school contexts. This chapter focuses on a number of key management and organisational issues across schools, whose importance and relevance cannot be underestimated. Using case-study data, the chapter looks at the focal role of the Transition Year Co-ordinator, staff involvement in the programme, the issue of staff development and in-service provision, the teaching methods employed in Transition Year and the resources available for the programme. The use of ability grouping and student assessment within Transition Year are also examined.

5.1 CO-ORDINATION AND STAFF INVOLVEMENT

> All members of the Transition Year team should be committed to the philosophy, aims and successful implementation of the Transition Year programme (Department of Education, 1993).

According to the mission statement, the success of Transition Year is contingent on the presence of a well-informed and interested staff who are aware of the objectives of Transition Year. The case-studies of schools allowed us to question management and teachers about co-ordination and staff involvement within Transition Year. It was evident in each of the case-study schools that the Transition Year Co-ordinator is pivotal in broadening the mission to include the whole school and staff.

Each of the case-study schools has a Transition Year Co-ordinator (TYC) who plays a central role in maintaining and overseeing the Transition Year programme.[7] The variation in approaches to appointing a programme co-ordinator was perhaps one of the most surprising differences among the case-study schools. In some schools, appointment of the Transition Year co-ordinator was based on staff interest in taking the post; this was particularly evident in Mt. Cook:

> I just showed an interest in doing it. . . . My main reason would be that I always had an emphasis towards the senior cycle. . . . I was one of the teachers who was focussed on that particular age group. I thought that was where my interest lay and then it developed from that (Transition Year Co-ordinator, Mt. Cook).

In other schools, the appointment was contingent on staff availability, a pattern that was particularly evident in Manners Mall, Cuba St. and Willis St. schools:

> The principal talked me into it basically and I agreed to give it a go and so here I am (TYC, Cuba St.).

> Interviewer: How did your appointment as co-ordinator come about?

> TYC: I was asked in the middle of the yard, would I like to do it (Willis St.).

> They [the Principal and deputy principal] decided I would be Transition Year Co-ordinator. . . . I just thought I was put in completely at the deep end. I was put in charge of Transition Year. I was given the post on a Friday. I started on the Monday and I didn't have anything [training]. I think that is really bad (TYC, Hopper St.).

A recurring theme among the Transition Year co-ordinators interviewed was the lack of time allocation for the work involved in co-ordination:

> I actually think myself if the co-ordinator is to do the job properly, he should have a reduction in hours that would allow the co-ordinator to make a real input into the content of what's being taught

---

[7] In one school, Victoria St., co-ordination was shared among two teachers.

in the different areas in TY, because I feel that I haven't the time for it (TYC, Cuba St.).

I think that if the TY programme is going to run you have got to give hours; two hours a week B post allowance is not enough if you want to run a really good programme. It's an awful lot of work. You need to monitor the students all the time. You need to be able to go around the class and talk to the students nearly every day with the various activities that are going on. You just don't have time for that if you have a full timetable as well (TYC, Hopper St.).

I don't think I have any specific time allocation this year, not that I am aware of. As I say, maybe the principal would differ on that. I certainly have a fairly full timetable compared to previous years (TYC, Mt. Cook).

Furthermore, as was evidenced by the TYCSS study (2000a), there was a good deal of variation across schools in the time allocated for the position of co-ordinator. In Manners Mall, for example, the co-ordinator was given two hours per week for the work involved while the co-ordinator in Victoria St. was unsure as to whether specific time had been allocated for the work.

The Transition Year Co-ordinator plays a key role in communicating with other staff members about the content and organisation of the programme. It was interesting to find that, in most cases, communication with other teachers depended on informal channels rather than set meetings with staff members:

We meet occasionally and sometimes it might just be a case of having a quick chat and that might do whatever we want to do (TYC, Willis St.).

It [contact with other TY teachers] would be more so when it involves, say, speakers and that. I suppose we [the TYCs] really would be the link between them all and we would meet. And I suppose share the information around that way. I suppose we have no formal sit-down but there would be a fair amount of communication that way (TYC, Victoria St.).

The point in this school is as teachers we meet each other so often that there is less need to meet formally. We tend to meet a lot of the

> time, informally say break time, lunch-time and then because we all
> eat together so we are meeting all the time so we can generally deal
> with things as we go. So we don't tend to formalise things too much
> (TYC, Mount Cook).

One of the co-ordinators felt that a reliance on informal contact allowed
insufficient time for programme development and co-ordination:

> When I have a free class or whenever I see teachers in the staff room
> or up the corridor or I call to them in their class or wherever it hap-
> pens to be. There isn't any specific time set aside and that is one of
> the big problems with it. . . . I talk to some of the teachers: "what are
> you doing, what are you at" and so forth and you get a certain
> amount of feedback. . . . But you need time to get them [teachers], to
> encourage them to take up new things and try new things. You don't
> have any time for that (TYC, Cuba St.).

Chapter Four has outlined the curricular content of the programme and
how it is often devised by a number of teachers rather than the Transition
Year co-ordinator alone. Similarly, in a number of the case-study
schools, management of the programme involves a Transition Year
committee. Schools vary in the extent to which a wider group of teachers
are involved in the running of the programme and it was evident that the
presence of a Transition Year Committee is very much contingent on the
level of interest among staff. Transition Year Committees, when in
place, are generally comprised of a co-ordinator along with class tutors
and/or the year head:

> There is a year head and then myself, the co-ordinator. We work to-
> gether. Mainly the Transition Year head would take care of any dis-
> cipline problems, attendance, that side of things and I would take
> care of activities and organising the programme basically for them
> outside their main subjects (TYC, Hopper St).

> It varies at different times of the year but . . . the year head and the
> career guidance counsellor would be involved (TYC, Willis St.).

> We would meet as tutors and the programme is developed with all
> four of us really, if you like the team that have developed the pro-
> gramme over time because they most heavily teach it (TYC, Mt.
> Cook).

However, teams varied in the extent to which they were seen as actively involved in management and co-ordination:

> My meetings would include two Transition Year class tutors and other class tutors, if you know what I mean. So, as such, there is no active core team and it's the one area that I'm hoping to kick off. I was hoping to kick it off this year but as of yet it hasn't kicked off (TYC, Wallace St.).

The existence of other teachers involved in the core team was seen as beneficial to the work of the co-ordinator:

> We have a teacher whose post is to look after work experience which is great, and that's certainly taken a lot of the administrative . . . pressure off me as co-ordinator. That is a very, very time consuming element on its own. To do it properly and to evaluate it, to make it a really worthwhile experience, . . . it does take somebody individually to do it (TYC, Mt. Cook).

It was evident in a number of schools that the presence of a Transition Year committee was often difficult to sustain. For example, teachers and management in Hopper St. and in Willis St. schools spoke of enthusiastic beginnings for such committees, enthusiasm which often ended up fading away over time:

> There is [a core team], yes. It has been more active, I suppose, in previous years. We haven't the need to get them involved, it varies at different times of the year but we have the year head and the career guidance counsellor would be involved (TYC, Willis St.).

> I think what happened was that the people's involvement became a bit more diluted. That group was very much active in designing the whole course and then I suppose people put in so much effort that year that they tended to apply their efforts in a more personal way to whatever they were teaching in TY. But as a committee it didn't really continue on through the years (Former TYC, Hopper St.).

> In the beginning there was high standards and constant meetings, but it's fizzled out in the last two years (Teacher, Hopper St.).

In Hopper St., in order to promote enthusiasm among staff for Transition Year, the principal and co-ordinator meet every day with staff meetings held once a month.

In some schools, staff members were seen to vary in terms of their attitude to Transition Year and hence in their willingness to get involved in running the programme:

> I wouldn't say there's a core team because some people express an interest and others don't want anything to do with it. If they are assigned it, they'll take it and if they're not, they are not going to be coming in here saying why I didn't get it (Principal, Victoria St.).

> You will find that some people are very negative towards it [TY] for various reasons (TYC, Cuba St.).

In addition to lack of interest, interviews with teachers revealed that additional commitments, other than teaching, often constrain time:

> You see there are so many new things coming in all the time on top of what schools are supposed to be doing which is teaching and you get these more able people and they are all taken and put doing other things so you are spreading yourself every way (TYC, Cuba St.).

These commitments include posts of responsibility, non-post administrative roles (such as class tutor) and extra-curricular activities outside of school. At least half of the teachers teaching Transition Year in Victoria, Cuba, Hopper and Wallace St. schools hold posts of responsibility. As a result, the Transition Year Co-ordinator is likely to have an increased workload in terms of management and liaison with teachers.

Teachers in the case-study schools were asked about the frequency of staff meetings relating to Transition Year. Again, there was a good deal of variation across schools. For example, in Manners Mall there are no formal meetings between core staff involved in Transition Year due to time and logistical constraints:

> I couldn't possibly introduce another meeting into the timetable, into the weekly timetable. It wouldn't take it because it is quite difficult as it is with the meetings we have scheduled into it because it restricts a huge number of teachers (Principal, Manners Mall).

In Hopper St., meetings had been specifically used to try to revitalise the Transition Year programme:

> We wanted to look at a couple of issues in the school and one of the issues we looked at very clearly was TY . . . we let off the kids three half days in a row and there were sets of meetings (Principal, Hopper St.).

In Mt. Cook, regular three-weekly meetings among the core team were supplemented with informal interaction with other staff members. In Wallace St., annual meetings are held to discuss the Transition Year programme:

> At the beginning of the year there is provision there where all the Transition Year teachers get an opportunity to meet and the TYC will spell out the objectives for the year and the main aims in terms of travels and all that sort of thing he would have all that organised (Principal, Wallace St.).

General staff meetings, usually held once a term, were also used to discuss Transition Year among other issues. Transition Year issues were generally well represented in general staff meetings, particularly in Hopper St., Willis St., Mount Cook and Manners Mall. However, intermediate structures, such as subject departments, were also seen as having an influence on the operation of the Transition Year programme in Mount Cook:

> The TYC would raise matters as co-ordinator but again in the core curriculum people are working in the context of their subject departments as it were and they're working on that basis. The people who are involved in the extension modules are doing what they want to do and they set about doing it (Principal, Mt. Cook).

Given that the success of the programme is seen as contingent on the interest and motivation among a wide group of teachers, it is interesting to see how some schools have all (or almost all) of their teachers teach Transition Year classes, while in other schools there is a choice. In Cuba St. and Mt. Cook, not all teachers were obliged to teach Transition Year students:

It's based on a combination of their willingness and the need. If a teacher says "I absolutely don't want anything to do with fourth year", I usually respect that (Principal, Cuba St.).

Generally speaking any new teachers would be given Transition Year classes. They can't say no I suppose. So you have core teachers that have always been teaching Transition Year, some that don't teach at all and then others that change every year or two and they will bring with them their own specific interests and therefore we can hone that in on the programme (TYC, Mt. Cook).

The disadvantage of this approach related to subject provision:

Now that hasn't actually always helped the programme in that certain subject areas aren't well covered (TYC, Mt. Cook).

In sum, variation was evident across the case-study schools in the development, management and day-to-day teaching of the Transition Year programme. In particular, lack of time for co-ordination activities and formal meetings among teachers emerged as difficulties in running the programme.

5.2 STAFF DEVELOPMENT AND IN-SERVICE PROVISION

According to the Department of Education guidelines (1993):

It will be a condition of participation in Transition Year programmes that schools will become involved in programmes of staff development/inservice education which will be locally and regionally based.

As a response, the Transition Year Curriculum Support Service (TYCSS) was established in 1998 to assist principals, Transition Year co-ordinators, core teams and the wider staff with various aspects of the programme, including planning and writing the programme. The TYCSS provides a team of teachers with experience of teaching and co-ordinating Transition Year programmes, available to schools for consultation and advice. The team also organises in-service training workshops within schools and for clusters of schools as well as co-operating with educational and other agencies in producing teaching and learning resources for Transition Year programmes.

Interviews with 142 teachers within the seven case-study schools allowed us to estimate the prevalence of participation in Transition Year related in-service training along with issues regarding in-service among teachers and management. Excluding Transition Year Co-ordinators, only a minority (28 per cent) of teachers teaching Transition Year had taken part in in-service relating to the programme while the majority (73 per cent) of teachers had taken part in other in-service in the previous three years. Participation in in-service relating to Transition Year varied somewhat across schools, ranging from a tenth of teachers in Manners Mall to over a third of teachers in Cuba St., Willis St. and Victoria St. Those teaching more "innovative" Transition Year subjects were somewhat more likely than those teaching traditional academic subjects to have taken part in in-service training (36 per cent compared with 22 per cent). A third of the teachers who received in-service described it as "very useful" with sixty per cent deeming it "useful".

In some schools, in-service training had been provided at a particular point of time, mainly around the inception of the programme but teachers who had subsequently begun teaching Transition Year had not received training:

> We have a lot of new teachers, a lot of them very young, who weren't involved in the original decision-making that developed towards the three-year Leaving Cert and I think it would be no harm if we all sat down for a day with proper guidance and to re-evaluate where we are going and to look at the aims and objectives again and maybe with a view to designing a course (TYC, Hopper St.).

> I think we have quite a number of new teachers this year and they haven't been through the same training processes. It is hard to know whether they have actual needs which may only establish during the school year so at the end of the year we suddenly find so-and-so had great difficulty with a particular area and then that will identify a need (TYC, Mt. Cook).

This is evidenced by the fact that those who have received Transition Year-related in-service have generally been teaching longer in the school than those who have not (an average of 17 years compared with 9 years respectively).

In spite of the lack of take-up of in-service training, a number of teachers stressed the need for training and support:

> Some in-service is definitely needed. Everyone does a good job but only one teacher knows what she's doing, and you only really learn through doing it (Teacher, Mt. Cook).

> We really need some in-service or cluster groups of teachers involved to pool ideas and come up with suggestions. I'm not aware of any in-service for TY music (Teacher, Mt. Cook).

> The work programmes are concrete and the materials are available, but other subjects such as science and maths are affected by a lack of materials and guidance in my view (Teacher, Wallace St.).

> We need more in-service. Just because something is running doesn't mean that it can run without care and attention. It runs in danger of being just another year (Teacher, Hopper St.).

In addition, the need for on-going in-service training to maintain enthusiasm for the Transition Year programme was seen as crucial:

> What we need is more in-service on a regular basis. It's a matter of keeping the interest up (Teacher, Hopper St.).

> What we need is more structure, more guidelines and an injection of new ideas (Teacher, Mt. Cook).

> Because the project is bigger than I had imagined, I would love some help of the kind I got before, a meeting about the stage we're at now and a couple of guidelines (Teacher, Hopper St.).

The need for training for the design and implementation of interdisciplinary courses was also mentioned:

> I think it [our training need] is mainly with the staff on how to interlink courses. There is not a lot of interdisciplinary work going on (Principal, Cuba St.).

As a result of the lack of take-up of in-service training, there had been little on-going contact between the case-study schools and the Transition Year support team. In such cases, teachers were very much dependent on each other to pass on ideas and skills:

I suppose we haven't felt the need really [to contact the support team], but I suppose we know it is there if we did need it. I would say a lot of the information they said to get was already here, like the Transition Year pack and all of that. So we had that, like I said the prior TYC initially handed over the books so we had her pieces there (TYC, Victoria St.).

Interviewer: Have you had any contact with the Transition Year support team yet?

TYC: Just they sent out literature to me and I have whatever the previous Transition Year co-ordinator had already (TYC, Hopper St.).

Because there is no textbook, it's difficult to work without guidelines. Help from the other teacher was invaluable (Teacher, Wallace St.).

We need better resources for teachers — more in-service. Teachers do help out each other and pass on notes (Teacher, Wallace St.).

As well as teachers, Transition Year Co-ordinators were questioned about the training that they had received upon appointment to the role. All Transition Year co-ordinators interviewed had received in-service training prior to, or early into, their appointment with the exception of the co-ordinator in Hopper St. In this case, there was no time to prepare for the new position given the short notice involved:

I have asked already because, as I say, I was given the post. It wasn't something that I applied for that I had done work on already. So I haven't had in-service as of yet (TYC, Hopper St.).

While it would seem that this co-ordinator had been unlucky due to timing, a former co-ordinator in Hopper St reported a similar experience, suggesting that the school management were not aware of the importance of training in facilitating the programme:

I did take part in some while I was doing it. Looking back it's a pity I couldn't have done it the year before but the year before I didn't know I was going to be the co-ordinator (Former TYC, Hopper St.).

A number of Transition Year Co-ordinators commented on the demands of the position and the importance of in-service training to meet these demands:

> You can drift away from the original aims and objectives of the Transition Year and just by touching base every now and then it [in-service] helps to draw you back on course and remember why it was set up and where you are meant to be heading (Former TYC, Hopper St.).

In sum, in-service training tends to be focused on Transition Year co-ordinators with only a minority of subject teachers taking part in such training. However, a number of teachers highlighted the need for such provision to contribute to the on-going development of the programme within their school.

5.3 Teaching Methods within Transition Year Classes

Chapter Four has outlined how the curriculum is decided and the content of the programme. This section focuses on the teaching methods employed in Transition Year. According to the Department guidelines:

> A key feature of Transition Year should be the use of a wide range of teaching/learning methodologies and situations. . . . Educational activities undertaken should enable students to have a valid and worthwhile learning experience with emphasis given to developing studying skills and self-directed learning.

The guidelines promote a departure from traditional teaching methods, highlighting the use of alternative materials and learning situations in an attempt to enhance self-directed learning. More detailed guidelines suggest that methods such as negotiated learning, activity-based learning, group work, project work, visiting speakers and day trips, to name just a few, could be used in teaching Transition Year modules.

Within the case-study schools, interviews with teachers were used to explore the kinds of methods they used in teaching Transition Year classes. Figure 5.1 indicates the extent to which particular approaches were used in every lesson or most lessons. The majority of teachers reported reinforcing basic skills in the subject area, introducing new topics and using a range of methods to approach the subject in a different way in every lesson or most lessons. A significant minority reported introducing Leaving Cert topics but many teachers reported that this related to the teaching of skills (for example, language skills) relevant to the broad Leaving Cert curriculum rather than to coverage of the specific syllabus. A quarter of teachers used the traditional approach whereby students copy notes from the board while a similar proportion used group or pair-work in class. There was little evidence of teachers co-operating with other teachers across subject boundaries[8] or allowing students to contribute to the content of lessons for every or most lessons. Interestingly, schools varied in the extent to which students influenced the content of some lessons with student-directed provision being more prevalent in Mt. Cook and Victoria St. schools.

Figure 5.1: Methods used in every/most lessons by Transition Year teachers

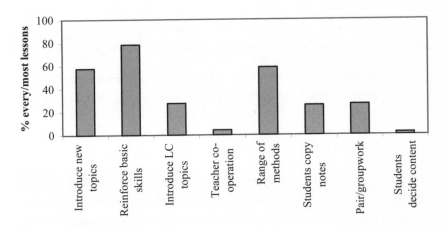

Source: Case studies of schools.

Interestingly, differences in methods between those teaching traditional academic subjects and those teaching "Transition Year" subjects are fewer than might be expected. Teachers of "innovative" subjects (that is,

---

[8] A number of the courses taught were interdisciplinary in nature (see Chapter Four) but this did not generally involve team teaching or similar forms of teacher co-operation.

subjects not usually provided within second-level education) are some-what more likely to report using a range of methods and more likely to report using visiting speakers and video/audiotapes than those teaching academic subjects. Among academic subject teachers, those teaching Irish, English and Maths are somewhat less likely to report using a range of methods and used pair- or group-work less frequently. However, it is important to note there is a diversity among teachers of all subject areas in the approach they use. A number of teachers stressed their reliance on practical activities when taking Transition Year classes:

> TY classes are easy to handle. It's very much hands-on, using visual aids and showing them how to do stuff (Art Teacher, Manners Mall).

> I want them to love the subject and I try to incorporate as much prac-tical work as possible which they mightn't have the time for next year (Biology Teacher, Hopper St.).

In addition, teachers attempted to promote student engagement in the subject:

> Communication is important. A lot of role play is used based on the various situations that students may find themselves in while in Spain, in a shop, restaurant or on a bus (Spanish Teacher, Mount Cook).

> I use open discussion, brainstorming to produce ideas (Business Studies Teacher, Mount Cook).

> [I use] a more interactive approach, we sit in a circle and it gives them a chance to express themselves, we discuss what comes up with them (Religion Teacher, Victoria St.).

Overall, half of those teaching Transition Year reported that their ap-proach with Transition Year students differs "a good deal" to that used with other senior cycle classes with a further quarter reporting that their approach differs "to some extent". The approach was seen to differ "a good deal" more frequently in Wallace St., Cuba St. and Victoria St. schools than in the other case-study schools. A significant minority (23 per cent) of those teaching academic subjects reported that their ap-proach did not differ from that used with other senior cycle classes. As might be expected, teachers who reported using a range of methods with

Transition Year classes were more likely to report that their approach differed a "good deal" from that used with other senior cycle classes (67 per cent compared with 34 per cent).

The kinds of methods used by Transition Year teachers were explored in greater detail within the case-study schools. A good deal of the discussion focused on the range of *materials* used rather than the diversity of *methods* per se. Materials used included books, class sets, videos, puzzles, slides, posters, fact sheets, specimens, projects, work sheets, photocopies, novels, short stories, tapes, newspaper articles, games, handouts, government reports and experiments. Under a quarter of teachers reported using textbooks as the main resource within Transition Year classes. As might be expected, those teaching academic subjects were more likely than those teaching "innovative" subjects to report using textbooks as the main method (31 per cent compared with 9 per cent); this pattern was more evident in Irish, English, Maths and European languages than in other subjects. This pattern can be attributed to a number of reasons, many of which were outlined by teachers. Some teachers mentioned the lack of suitable textbooks:

> We have no set text — I never found a satisfactory book so we just use particular sections of other books. I bring up other interesting material such as songs and poetry (Irish Teacher, Mount Cook).

Others outlined the unnecessary expense of students obtaining textbooks for one year (especially if students may not be continuing the subject into Leaving Cert):

> We have no textbook. It's too expensive to buy school books if they are not necessary, so we use our own resources (Science Teacher, Willis St.).

Additionally, some teachers felt that there is no need for textbooks in Transition Year and preferred to adapt other resources for use in class:

> We have no set textbooks, I give the students various handouts of poetry, short stories, novel extracts and so on. I use a number of cut-outs from articles (English Teacher, Victoria St.).

> In Maths we try to stay as far away from the standard curriculum so we use computers and spreadsheets a lot (Maths Teacher, Wallace St.).

> I use a mix of traditional chalk and talk with more discussion and more exploration of author and poets' lives . . . emphasising reading for enjoyment and acquisition of current affairs knowledge (English Teacher, Victoria St.).

> I use a workshop approach — problems and issues are identified and solved through the accounting system (Accountancy Teacher, Willis St).

> While we have books, we don't use them that much, we have videos and other stuff like puzzles (Irish Teacher, Manners Mall).

However, the interviews suggest that a number of teachers use the same materials as used in the Leaving Certificate:

> In Maths it's very much left up to yourself, and we use bits from different books. In Irish we use the same textbook for fifth year (Maths and Irish Teacher, Willis St.).

> I teach a pass class so we pick on stuff from the Junior Cert which is also covered in Leaving Cert. Sometimes we use Junior Cert books and then move on to more difficult topics such as algebra (Maths Teacher, Willis St.).

It was also evident in a number of schools that teachers use a "learn as you go" approach to selecting the various teaching materials and methods:

> The materials used varies, some years we might try something and then scrap it (French Teacher, Hopper St.).

Many of the teachers emphasised the time without examination pressure afforded by Transition Year; this was seen as giving teachers scope to introduce a more varied approach to teaching methods:

> We have more time to explore things that we can't with an exam syllabus (Maths Teacher, Manners Mall).

> While it's not always a very different approach, we always try to make it more interesting for students and give a bit more time for discussion (Science Teacher, Victoria St.).

> We're not bounded by a course exam and I can do things that I like, pupils will pick up on that and that's the biggest advantage of TY (Irish Teacher, Wallace St.).

For other teachers, Transition Year meant less pressure but otherwise the methods used remained similar to those used with other year groups:

> It's not radically different but we do have time to do things, otherwise you would continue to have the pressure of the Leaving Cert syllabus (English Teacher, Cuba St.).

> The approach doesn't differ enormously but there is less pressure and considerably less written work. The topic is much the same (English Teacher, Manners Mall).

> The materials are not different, but there's not as much pressure in the classroom. The way I teach is very much the same (Physics Teacher, Hopper St.).

In sum, Transition Year is used by teachers to reinforce basic skills and introduce new topics to students. Most teachers report using a wider range of methods than they use with other senior cycle classes. Transition Year teachers tend to use a range of different materials and resources in class, with only a minority having a strong reliance on textbooks. However, a significant minority of teachers, especially in the more academic subjects, continue to use a more traditional "talk and chalk" approach.

5.4 RESOURCES USED IN TRANSITION YEAR

A range of resources are available for Transition Year. The Department of Education and Science provides a special grant to schools per student participating which may be used for any expenses relating exclusively to the Transition Year programme.[9] As explained in Chapter Four, there is no prescribed curriculum for Transition Year, but there are a number of

---

[9] In 2002/3, the additional grant per Transition Year student was €63.50; at the same time, the per capita grant for all (non-disadvantaged) schools in the free education scheme was €266.49 (Department of Education and Science Circular M71/01; Circular M31/02).

departmental and Transition Year Support Team Service booklets and information outlining guidelines in the form of a Resource Pack. While the resource material is not prescriptive, it is intended as a resource for whole-school development and enrichment of programmes offered by schools. In addition to the work of the Support Service, regular monitoring and external evaluation of the Transition Year Programme is the responsibility of the Department of Education and Science's inspectorate and psychological service. Each school must have a clearly documented programme approved by its board of management.

Teachers in the case-study schools were asked about their level of satisfaction with the resources available to them in Transition Year. Teachers were divided on the issue. On the one hand, a number of teachers expressed satisfaction with the material resources available to them, albeit stressing the importance of their own efforts in building up such resources:

> I have a lot of support, anything I want I get, not a problem (Geography Teacher, Wallace St.).

> The resources are quite good, I collected stuff over the years for my subject. It's an easy department and well resourced, we have a good video library and students get a new handout in practically every lesson (Local Studies Teacher, Wallace St.).

> I am very satisfied. If I missed something such as materials, I would get 100 per cent co-operation from the Principal. I have completed a lot of work on this myself (Engineering Teacher, Hopper St.).

On the other hand, a number of teachers were not aware of the resources available or were dissatisfied with existing resources:

> We have no specific resources, we use stuff from the Art room. The students do brilliant work for Interior Design. It's a subject that they love and because of effort they put in I would like to give them more of an award (Design Teacher, Cuba St.).

> The Department doesn't provide resources for Maths teachers (Maths Teacher, Mt. Cook).

Other schools cited the need for material resources such as more funding, the need for computers and modes of transport for the school:

> Resources are very limited, the girls themselves provide the resources and access to computers and transport is very limited (Business Studies Teacher, Victoria St.).

> I would like more computer facilities. Space is a big issue and time-tabling (Maths Teacher, Manners Mall).

A recurrent theme in the interviews suggests that time is an important resource needed by Transition Year co-ordinators, teachers and management alike:

> Most of the resources come from ourselves. It takes a huge amount of time. There are no resources and that makes it costly and time-consuming. TY would be a flop without doing that, it's so poorly financed (Religion Teacher, Willis St.).

> We need more time, we don't need more physical resources (English Teacher, Hopper St.).

It is felt that, due to pressing curricular duties as well as additional administrative responsibilities, teachers lack the time to carry out all the duties which are entailed in teaching a Transition Year class:

> They [the teachers] are also supposed, according to the Department, to draw up a kind of a more detailed summary of their course and that's supposed to be kept here in the book where the Department can look at it and so forth. . . . Yet only a minority of individuals have actually done it. Now they haven't time either (TYC, Cuba St.).

Teachers also felt that more time with other teachers was important for the planning of cross-curricular activities and the overall direction of the programme:

> We need more time given to meeting with other TY teachers, more cross-curricular activity (Religion Teacher, Manners Mall).

> [We need] more time for meetings between teachers, a lot of the rest is informal, and more contact between tutors (Irish Teacher, Hopper St.).

Interviewer: What resources would you like to see in place?

Teacher: Having TY (subject) meetings once a month. . . . It's very pressurized for what has to be done (SPHE Teacher, Hopper St.).

Surprisingly, given the support mechanisms in place, some teachers mentioned a problem in obtaining support. It seems that some teachers may not be aware of the support supplied by the TYCSS or they may feel they require more specific support than that offered:

Outside there's nothing available, such as class plans. It's difficult to come up with resources. We have no concise resources to use within class (SPHE Teacher, Mt. Cook).

Initially I would have liked to go to courses — I couldn't find them (IT Teacher, Hopper St.).

I feel that there should be a network of workshops, and guest speakers to circulate in schools, especially for TY (Physics Teacher, Hopper St.).

Other teachers suggested that they would like to obtain additional information from these support systems:

I would like to see a TY support unit. In the early days there was contact, but we could do with some in-service regarding an Irish workshop (Irish Teacher, Willis St.).

They could prepare a LCA–type backup service which could take a more proactive role in the school and come in once a year (Business Studies Teacher, Willis St.).

We need ideas (not guidelines) because schools vary (Maths/Science Teacher, Willis St.).

While teachers mainly identified the importance of both material and teaching resources, school management was generally more concerned with the allocation of finance and teachers to Transition Year. The Principal of Wallace St., a very large school, feels that a major resource needed is more teachers to accommodate such large Transition Year classes. The Principal of this school states:

> Now in the normal mainstream situation you could put thirty in a class but if you put thirty into a Transition Year class it's too hard to handle with the flexibility and the way the actual classes are run. Thirty are too many, twenty-four is acceptable but you have the situation where we break the two classes into three for options so that is soaking up our resources in terms of teacher allocation.

A Transition Year Co-ordinator outlined how such a scenario can affect the day-to-day life of a Transition Year student:

> We always need more teachers particularly if you have an outing that you have [to have] more people available (TYC, Mt. Cook).

As might be expected, resource needs also depend on student intake and school characteristics. For example, the Principals in both Wallace St. and Cuba St. schools, both serving more working-class populations, highlighted the need for learning support and remediation resources. The Principal of Victoria St. outlined the need for more space, while the TYC of Hopper St. called for more in-service among teachers.

In general, the major resource constraint for the running of the Transition Year programme was seen to be time. In addition, a number of teachers were not aware of, or unable to access, resources from the support services.

5.5 ABILITY GROUPING IN TRANSITION YEAR

The use of ability grouping is a contentious issue within educational circles, with ongoing debate about the impact of streaming on academic achievement and other student outcomes (see, for example, Ireson and Hallam, 2001; Smyth, 1999). However, to date, little attention has been given to the prevalence of ability grouping in Transition Year. Among the seven case-study schools, three schools group students by ability[10] in structuring base classes in Transition Year, generally as a continuation from junior cycle. In these schools, ability grouping in Transition Year was made feasible by the large cohort of students taking the programme: in Willis and Hopper St., participation in Transition Year was "quasi-

---

[10] The approach used is "banding" (that is, having two or more "higher" or "lower" classes) rather than strictly hierarchical streaming.

compulsory", with a high level of voluntary participation among students in Victoria St. The decision to group Transition Year classes by ability was not clearly related to the academic ethos of the school; two of these schools were academic in orientation with higher average exam grades (Willis and Victoria St. schools) while the other school tended to have somewhat lower academic performance (Hopper St. school). In addition, in two other schools (Cuba St. and Mt. Cook), students were grouped by ability for some subjects, usually Irish, English or Maths.

Teachers were asked about the advantages and disadvantages of ability grouping within Transition Year. The advantages of grouping were stressed to a greater extent by those teaching Irish, English and Maths. Firstly, a number of teachers commented that grouping by ability is beneficial for students as they all work at different levels and so their progress is enhanced:

> It's very good to stream, they're all progressing at an equal pace (IT Teacher, Hopper St.).

> In Maths you have honours and pass classes on the basis of Junior Certificate results. It's less rigid as to who wants to do honours this year but the big advantage of having them streamed is that they all work at a different pace and a different level (Maths Teacher, Willis St.).

> Students are streamed for Irish. It's the only sure way to give everyone a chance (Irish Teacher, Mt. Cook.).

> By streaming, brighter students can get on better, have more challenging homework and in other groups, performance is better. It's better all round for everyone (Religion Teacher, Hopper St.).

Secondly, a number of teachers considered that ability grouping resulted in less class disruption and a better work ethic for (some) students. This was particularly emphasised by teachers in Hopper St.:

> The advantage of streaming students for Maths is that students have a more serious approach to Transition Year (Maths Teacher, Hopper St.).

> Students are streamed according to their previous results. I think that it's very good that students are streamed as the mixed ability wasn't

working. You would get disruptive students mixed in with bright students and that held back the class (Religion Teacher, Hopper St.).

Thirdly, a number of teachers considered that it is easier to teach students when all at the same level and ability, especially when in large groups:

Maths classes are streamed based on Junior Certificate results. It's very necessary in Maths, you couldn't teach the different levels. They follow a programme geared for their level (Maths Teacher, Mt. Cook.).

Students are streamed for English and rather than having them mixed, it's easier to teach (English Teacher, Hopper St.).

Students are streamed for Maths, I would insist upon it, you're caught between ordinary, pass and higher students, so they are divided into three groups this year (Maths Teacher, Victoria St.).

Students are streamed for Maths and the advantages outweigh the disadvantages. We can teach them at the level that they are at. If the class is mixed it makes it more difficult as honours and pass are very different courses (Maths Teacher, Willis St.).

However, a number of teachers outlined disadvantages associated with grouping Transition Year students by ability. The main arguments centred on the negative effects in terms of academic motivation and labelling students, especially less advantaged students:

Students are banded and it's a disadvantage at the bottom level — students are more turned off. They're more motivated if they're in with a few good lads (Maths Teacher, Willis St.).

It's best if students are mixed at this level, then you get a chance to see their ability. It's too early to split them — you're labelled then. It also challenges the more relaxed ones (English Teacher, Mount Cook).

Additionally, some staff in schools stressed the advantages of not streaming by ability for the student and the teacher:

Students are not streamed for English and they range from foundation to higher level material which makes choosing the material more difficult but perhaps it give students more confidence, especially orally (English Teacher, Victoria St.).

I would prefer mixed ability . . . The very academic kids have an opportunity to mix with the lower academic kids (Business Studies Teacher, Victoria St.).

TY is not exam-based, it encourages students who are weaker academically to strive to do better (Media Studies Teacher, Wallace St.).

I don't know why students are streamed, because it doesn't really work. Mixed ability is more advantageous to all concerned and it's more satisfying for the teacher (Religion Teacher, Hopper St.).

In general, arguments for and against ability grouping in Transition Year echoed those given by teachers of other year groups in previous research studies (see Smyth, 1999; Smyth et al., 2004). On the one hand, streaming was seen as facilitating a more appropriate pace of instruction for students. On the other hand, it was seen by some teachers as labelling students in a negative way with consequent difficulties in terms of student motivation. The extent to which ability grouping impacts on student attitudes to Transition Year is discussed in Chapter Seven below.

5.6 STUDENT ASSESSMENT WITHIN TRANSITION YEAR

According to Departmental guidelines, assessment within Transition Year is important in that it should be:

diagnostic to provide accurate information with regard to pupil strengths and weaknesses, and formative so as to facilitate improved pupil performance through effective programme planning and implementation.

Previous research has highlighted the diversity of approaches to assessment across different schools (Department of Education, 1996). Variation in assessment methods was evident among the case-study schools, although all schools assess Transition Year students at some point over the school year.

A variety of approaches to assessment was used by teachers, including portfolios, credit system, project work, homework, class tests, activity diaries, worksheets, self-assessment, quizzes and other assignments. Forty-one per cent of subject teachers reported giving their students regular homework. The approach to homework varied across schools with regular homework more prevalent in Hopper St., Cuba St. and Victoria St. schools. Furthermore, over half (51 per cent) of those teaching academic subjects gave regular homework compared with less than a quarter (23 per cent) of those teaching "innovative" subjects. Regular homework was more a feature of Irish, English, Maths and language teaching than in other academic subjects.

The central role of the subject teacher in deciding their own approach to assessment was highlighted by a number of Transition Year Co-ordinators:

> Where the teacher is highly interested in the whole concept of Transition Year, they will develop a means of assessment where appropriate . . . for others they wouldn't bother too much and they may not set them regular work (TYC, Mount Cook).

> It's more or less left up to individual teachers. Some of them give projects to do and assess them on the basis of projects. Others give them small exams (TYC, Cuba St.).

> Assessment is very much up to the teacher. A lot of times the more academic subjects, such as Maths, will nearly have to be assessed, written down or done that way (TYC, Victoria St.).

It was interesting to find that, as well as regular homework, examination assessment, especially in the form of term exams, was more common among teachers of traditional academic subjects, a pattern that was evident across all schools. It was found that term examinations and term assessment were particularly evident in Willis St.:

> [They get] class tests once a month and mid-term and Christmas tests (Maths Teacher, Willis St.).

> They sit a formal Christmas examination which is subject based and again at the summer. Now some theorists will see that as being against the spirit of TY — I would have my own views on that. Teachers are getting them going on assignments, nevertheless ex-

aminations give them a focus and keep parents happy too (Principal, Willis St.).

In contrast, continuous assessment was more evident in Victoria St. and Mount Cook:

> [There is] assessment after each topic covered. This is a vital as language learning is block building and it must be verified that each layer is laid (Spanish Teacher, Mount Cook).

However, even within these schools, there was variation among subject teachers with traditional teachers in Victoria St. relying more on exams while innovative teachers in Willis St. used continuous assessment:

> They receive tests at the end of each chapter as well as Christmas and Summer exams (Maths Teacher, Victoria St.).

> It's a year when they're outside the main, they're learning skills to enable and help them in fifth and sixth year. They get project work and it's just a fantastic year. Assessment should be part and parcel of it, and they should be rewarded for initiative (IT Teacher, Willis St.).

Other teachers used alternative forms of assessment such as student ability to learn and their personal progress throughout the year:

> Reliability, attitude, ability to work with others and independent work also. At the end they hand up a document and evaluation — presentation is important (Business Studies Teacher, Cuba St.).

> There's no required assessment. We get personal feedback and give them a questionnaire for self-assessment (SPHE Teacher, Manners Mall).

> We keep a record of their work rate in class, behaviour and attendance, as well as the quality of their work within class and how materials are used (Religion Teacher, Wallace St.).

> There's no formal exam. They research a topic and present information informally through class time (Speechcraft Teacher, Victoria St.).

> The TYO organises on-going assessment and she also does an interview with them at the end of the year — a pretty in-depth interview

about their experiences and also really I suppose that is very much the assessment at the end of the year. It is to see how they have enjoyed it and how they have matured. And she usually involves maybe the guidance counsellor or myself or the deputy principal (Principal, Manners Mall).

In a number of cases, a range of methods of assessment are used:

Effort in class, required work regardless of standard, participation in class (Design Teacher, Cuba St.).

It varies from subject to subject. A lot of the courses are project-oriented so the assessment is based really on the finished project. Some people in the core subjects like to have their occasional tests so it will vary (Principal, Mount Cook).

They have projects which they are assessed on and they are graded on. They are also graded on their behaviour and attitude as well. They might not be given a percentage for their behaviour but they would be sent out in a report at Christmas and then summer. There is continuous assessment. It is not exam based (TYC, Hopper St.).

A mixture of approaches was particularly evident in Wallace St. where a credit system was in play. This gives all teachers the opportunity to assess all students according to academic performance, personal development and behaviour. It was perceived by teachers as motivating Transition Year students:

At least there was some way of assessing it and at the end of the year some way of crediting the students where before it was very much down to a marking system which again, in the nature of the programme itself, because it is so varied and so difficult because of the different projects and things like that for a teacher. It works very, very well. The TYC is totally in tune with it and the students understand it very well and it is very much together (Principal, Wallace St.).

Some [students] treat it as a doss year, so if you don't finish the work, you don't get credits (Art Teacher, Wallace St.).

Portfolios and project work also played a large part in the assessment procedure in Victoria St. and Hopper St., although other forms of assessment were also used:

> We use all three: formal exams, project-work and portfolios (English Teacher, Victoria St.).

> The approach taken to assessment would be that each module and each unit would be assessed — it would be the same as any other year, other than exam years, in the sense that they would be assessed at the end of the year. It assesses people's efforts as well. It's not just a conventional assessment. There are a number of strands to it and they would be rated along that (Principal, Hopper St.).

Upon completion of Transition Year, a number of schools awarded their students with an overall certificate. This was particularly emphasised in Wallace St., Victoria St., Cuba St., Willis St. and Manners Mall. In the case of Willis St. and Wallace St., students were differentiated based on their performance in Transition Year while this was not the case in Manners Mall:

> Basically, there are three types of cert. you can get, there is excellent, merit, and participation but there is no actual grading on it as such but depending on their contribution during the year as to which one they would get. It's their general performance during the year (TYC, Willis St.).

> They receive a cert. with either Pass, Merit or Distinction or a certificate of attendance for those who haven't reached the Pass rate. . . . So on the report going home I will have written on it Fail, Pass, Merit, Distinction for the parents . . . and I will call the parents in whose sons or daughters are below the pass mark and try and give them a jizz up. Because if we leave it to the end of the year it leaves it wide open for parents to come in and say why wasn't I informed that he wasn't doing well? And we had no way of quantifying it before whereas the credit system gives us a chance to do that. It's a bit more work, a lot more work for me in compiling this and going through it but I think it's worthwhile (Transition Year co-ordinator, Wallace St.).

> A report is given at Christmas and at the end of the year; this is based on teacher comments not grades. Students also have a folder

with their work in it and are assessed on the basis of their participation. At the end of the year, students are given the Department cert and a school cert with the subjects they have taken (but no grades); any external certs (e.g. on coaching) they are given are included alongside this (TYC, Manners Mall).

This was also the case in Mount Cook, but only exceptional students are recognised to be worthy of a certificate:

> There has been no absolute form of certification. It [TY] is partly seen as something that they have to do anyway, . . . you don't necessarily have to give every certificate to see the value of it. What we have done and we didn't do it last [year] . . . for various reasons is those students we felt made a particular positive participation did something positive then we gave a special certificate to those few (TYC, Mount Cook).

In Victoria St., and Cuba St. schools, students are presented with their certificates at a graduation service:

> They have a formal exam in the Summer and at Christmas time — a formal written exam and then we'll say something like Speech Craft, they will be assessed by the teacher and as part of the graduation they would get a big wad of certificates but a lot would be assessed by the teacher (Principal, Victoria St.).

> We give them certificates in various areas to try and encourage them. [They get them] at the end of the year, last year we had a kind of a presentation (TYC, Cuba St.).

> They receive certificates at the end of each term based upon their work at the electives. We try to work very heavily on reward on working the positive end of the street in terms of student motivation so there would be certificates along the way and then there would be awards (Principal, Cuba St.).

In keeping with previous research (Department of Education, 1996), variation was apparent across the case-study schools in the assessment methods used in Transition Year. There was a greater reliance on traditional methods such as homework and exams among teachers of academic subjects. However, many teachers attempted to assess students' "softer" skills, such as class participation and interpersonal skills. In some instances, students themselves were encouraged to engage in self-assessment, evaluating their progress throughout the year.

5.7 CONCLUSIONS

This chapter has highlighted some of the processes shaping the day-to-day operation of Transition Year programmes. One of the main issues highlighted by Transition Year Co-ordinators and subject teachers was the lack of time available for programme planning and co-operation among teachers. This is seen to have implications both for the workload of co-ordinators and for the potential to develop an interdisciplinary approach to Transition Year teaching.

Take-up of in-service training and support currently appears to centre on co-ordinators with only a minority of subject teachers receiving training relating to Transition Year. Where teachers do receive such training, it tends to take place at the time when the programme is introduced into the school. However, there is a felt need on the part of teachers for access to longer term support in developing the programme overall and courses in their specific subjects in particular.

In keeping with the spirit of Transition Year, many teachers adopt innovative methods to teaching and assessing Transition Year students. However, a significant minority of subject teachers, particularly those teaching academic subjects, adopt quite traditional methods, with a reliance on textbooks, regular homework and formal examinations.

The way in which these operational issues affect the perceived success of the Transition Year programme is discussed in the following chapters.

Chapter Six

SCHOOL MANAGEMENT AND TEACHER PERCEPTIONS OF TRANSITION YEAR

INTRODUCTION

This chapter draws from in-depth qualitative interviews with school management and teachers to explore perceptions of the Transition Year programme. The first section begins by looking at the perceived success of the programme in terms of a range of dimensions, including personal and social skills development, academic performance, reducing drop-out, and enhancing awareness of Leaving Cert subject choice and longer-term career options. The second section highlights what are seen as positive aspects of the programme by management and teachers while the extent to which Transition Year is seen as appropriate for all students is discussed in section three. Section four explores recommendations for changes within the Transition Year programme, as outlined by teachers and school management in the case-study schools.

6.1 PERCEIVED SUCCESS OF THE TRANSITION YEAR PROGRAMME

In the postal survey, principals in schools currently providing Transition Year were asked about their perceptions regarding the success of Transition Year in relation to a number of dimensions. Almost all principals saw the programme as very successful in promoting the personal development of the student (see Figure 6.1). The programme was seen as very successful in facilitating social skills development by over three-quarters of school principals while two-thirds felt that Transition Year was very successful in providing students with guidance in terms of subject choice

for Leaving Certificate. Over half saw the enhancement of career awareness as very successful while Transition Year was perceived as being
"somewhat successful" in promoting academic performance and reducing drop-out from school by over half of the principals surveyed.

***Figure 6.1: Perceived success of the Transition Year programme (% of
principals regarding it as "very successful")***

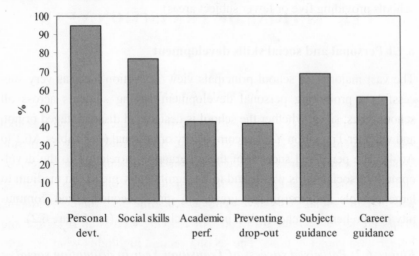

Source: Survey of School Principals (2001).

A composite measure of perceived success was derived by summing the
scores for these separate dimensions. Some variation was evident by type
of school in the perceived success of the Transition Year programme.
Principals of girls' secondary schools were more likely than those in
other school types to see the programme as successful with those in
boys' secondary and vocational schools viewing Transition Year as
somewhat less successful (see Table A6.1). In addition, principals in larger schools were somewhat more likely than those in smaller schools to
see the programme as very successful across a range of dimensions (Table A6.2). Furthermore, those in disadvantaged schools were less likely
to see the programme as successful (Table A6.3). Success ratings were
higher in schools where Transition Year is optional than in schools
where it is compulsory (Table A6.4). Schools which had introduced the
programme in the last six years are less likely to deem the programme as

very successful than schools with a longer-standing Transition Year (Table A6.5). This pattern may reflect initial "teething" problems associated with introducing the programme or alternatively only programmes deemed successful may be continued in schools over a longer term period. Success ratings were significantly higher in schools with broader Transition Year programmes than in those with more restricted programmes (2.67 in schools providing eight or more subject areas compared with 2.55 in schools providing five or fewer subject areas).

6.1.1 Personal and social skills development

The vast majority of school principals view Transition Year as very successful in promoting personal development among students across all school types, sizes, whether the school is designated disadvantaged or not, and whether Transition Year is compulsory or optional (see Tables A6.1 to A6.4). The perceived success of the programme in relation to the development of social skills was found to be significantly greater in medium to large schools and marginally greater in girls' secondary and community/comprehensive schools than in other school types (see Figure 6.2).

Figure 6.2: Perceived success of Transition Year in promoting social skills development (% of principals regarding it as "very successful")

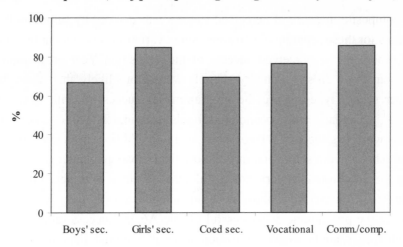

Source: Survey of School Principals (2001).

Interviews with school management and teachers in the case-study schools explored in greater depth the perceived success of Transition Year in promoting personal and social development among students. A main theme which emerged from the interviews was the role of Transition Year in enhancing maturity among students. A number of teachers outlined how Transition Year students could be clearly distinguished from non-participants in this regard:

> There's no doubt, an increased maturity in fifth year would be commented on by the students themselves because I'd know that from individual interviews with them, the ones who have done Transition year (Guidance Counsellor, Willis St.).

> TY has a maturing effect on some, especially boys; they're better able to make subject choices, wiser choices, [they are] more aware. They can cope better with senior cycle (Transition Year Co-ordinator, Manners Mall).

In particular, Transition Year was seen as enhancing student self-confidence and organisational skills:

> For this year . . . I think it's good. I think they are coming out of themselves. My class anyway are more confident. They are more willing to take responsibility and get things done, decide this is what I'm going to do and I'll organise this and they are good at delegating. I think it is very good for them (Transition Year Co-ordinator, Hopper St.).

> They certainly gain maturity. We have had a number of students who blossomed from it, there is no doubt; students who maybe went in quite shy or unfocused or went in for a doss year and emerged with a very different outlook on school life themselves (Guidance Counsellor, Wallace St.).

> Just from my own experience, even this year, just the girls I would have taught last year and seen how they have come out of themselves this year. And one girl in particular she . . . wouldn't stay quiet, but now she will keep quiet. . . . She seems to be more able to express herself (TY Co-ordinator, Victoria St.).

> Transition Year makes them very confident. The TY students have always done extremely well and come out on top. It's to do with confidence (Teacher, Victoria St.).

> I would say the opportunity to see themselves in a freer situation and to identify skills that they never thought they had. . . . They get opportunities to come forward so the leaders come forward as well. They may not be the brightest academically but they do have the social skills to manage and that in itself gives them tremendous confidence (Principal, Wallace St.).

Staff also identified areas of the programme that are particularly effective in developing personal and social skills. Key aspects of the programme include work-related learning, such as work experience placements and mini-company modules:

> The work experience I think is very good for them. It gives them an insight into where they work (Transition Year Co-ordinator, Hopper St.).

> As a result of Transition Year, they have a much broader outlook. The mini-company really lets them know what it's like to manage for themselves. It gives them a good view on life and jobs (Teacher, Mount Cook).

The survey of teachers in the seven case-study schools revealed that the majority of teachers across all schools felt that Transition Year was either "successful" or "very successful" in promoting the development of personal and social skills among students. Ratings were higher in Victoria St. and Manners Mall schools and somewhat lower in Hopper St. and Cuba St. schools. A very small number of teachers saw the programme as "very unsuccessful" in this respect. For the latter teachers, the lack of success of the programme was seen in the context of a lack of interest on the part of students or the lack of focus on personal development modules in the Transition Year programme:

> Some students use it as a doss year. If they're motivated they get a lot out of it such as self-development and self-confidence, for others it's a waste of time (Teacher, Wallace St.).

> Personal Development is not really done here (Teacher, Cuba St.).

Finally, while teachers relayed parental fears of students being "left be-hind" in terms of coping with the workload in fifth year, a number of principals and key personnel saw students' enhanced personal develop-ment as giving them the maturity to better engage with the Leaving Cert programme after taking part in Transition Year. These were typical comments:

> I think the majority of students are much more mature when they come back to fifth year. That doesn't mean that they are all good lit-tle boys . . . but, contrary to parental fears, they do get down to doing their work (Principal, Willis Street).

> I think they are going to mature because they are a year older and I think that stands to them when the pressure comes on in the main Leaving Cert (Principal, Victoria St.).

In general, school principals and teachers tended to regard the Transition Year programme as having a positive impact on personal and social de-velopment among students. Their accounts emphasised greater student maturity and self-confidence, traits that were also seen as contributing to subsequent Leaving Cert performance.

6.1.2 Academic performance

The majority of principals deemed Transition Year to be at least "some-what successful" in promoting academic performance. This pattern var-ied by school type; a smaller proportion of principals in vocational and community/comprehensive schools deemed it to be "very successful" compared with principals in girls' secondary schools (Figure 6.3). Prin-cipals in larger schools were somewhat more likely to see the pro-gramme as successful in academic terms, although the difference is not statistically significant (Table A6.2). Interestingly, those in disadvan-taged schools are less likely to view Transition Year as very successful in promoting academic performance than those in other school types (Table A6.3). There was no relationship between the perceived academic success of the programme and the breadth of the programme.

Figure 6.3: Perceived success of Transition Year in promoting academic performance (% of principals regarding it as "very successful")

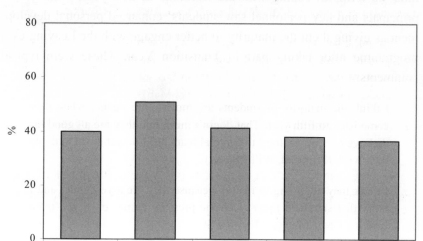

Source: Survey of School Principals (2001).

A similar pattern of findings emerged from the survey of teachers in the case-study schools, with over half of the teachers interviewed deeming the promotion of academic performance to have been either very successful or successful. However, there was some variation across schools with the highest success ratings in Willis St., Victoria St. and Wallace St. schools and somewhat lower ratings in Cuba St. school.

In a number of the case-study schools, Transition Year was seen to have a positive influence on academic performance, irrespective of school factors or the academic ability of the student:

> Interviewer: How successful do you think it [TY] has been in promoting academic performance?

> Principal: Very good, the kids that I think of when we talk about such things are the students at the extremes, the students who are weak, it gets them on board (Principal, Cuba St.).

> The best students are those who have done Transition Year (Teacher, Wallace St.).

It was evident across schools that reinforcement and revision of Junior Certificate material as well as some preparation of Leaving Certificate material was a major aid in developing academic performance:

> I think it has helped to promote academic performance. It is an extra year of English, Irish, Maths and I think it has helped. I know that some of the best results we have got in this school have come from students who did TY (Principal, Manners Mall).

> The extra time and experience does help in the subject (Teacher, Wallace St.).

On the other hand, a number of teachers pointed out that in order for students to benefit from Transition Year, they must be willing and eager to learn:

> Well it depends on the year. I have seen students who have shown potential and they were helped by the fact that they participated in that year, and they have done well in their Leaving Cert. Now who is to say they wouldn't have done well anyway because they would have had the potential. I think . . . basically you get out of it what you put into it. Like if you have an enthusiastic, receptive student I think they can benefit unbelievably (Guidance Counsellor, Manners Mall.).

> What the student puts into it the student gets out of it (Teacher, Wallace St.).

However, a number of teachers considered that certain groups of students did not benefit academically from Transition Year. This was seen as particularly evident among students who require a more structured approach to learning and those who are not interested or motivated by Transition Year:

> Some students get out of the habit of learning, and you really reap what you sow. If a student feels that there is no exam there's no emphasis on them to do things. They have a laid-back attitude and they don't benefit (Teacher, Cuba St.).

> It's very beneficial for some and very detrimental for others. Some kids really blossom not being lumbered with a curriculum. Others lose out – some don't like the idea of doing Transition Year and they

want to get out of school ASAP. For some it takes them away and
for others it takes them back (Teacher, Mount Cook).

Transition Year can have good effects on some. But many make the
wrong decision, especially because they're young, and if they're not
willing to put in the time and effort (Teacher, Wallace St.).

Some teachers stressed the difficulties experienced by less academically
able students who take Transition Year:

Promoting academic performance is about promoting a better work
ethic, but it really depends on the type of student. I feel that the more
able group really benefit from it (Teacher, Cuba St.).

Transition Year can have an adverse effect on weak students and
they can lose their way and their direction. It isn't suitable for some
pupils — it distracts them from some of the core subjects (Teacher,
Mount Cook).

A number of teachers perceived that the development of academic performance was not central to the Transition Year programme. Others felt
that because the nature of Transition Year is removed somewhat from
the Leaving Certificate curriculum that it could not have any great impact on academic performance:

It's not really an issue here. There is a programme set and it certainly
has nothing to do with the Leaving Certificate programme (Guidance
Counsellor, Willis St.).

It's not a very academic year, it's not supposed to be! (Teacher, Victoria St.).

In sum, while Transition Year was seen as having a broadly positive effect on academic performance, this was not seen as a central concern of
the programme. A number of teachers highlighted the potential difficulties associated with participation for less academically able students.

6.1.3 Reducing school drop-out

The Transition Year programme was seen to be successful in reducing
student drop-out in a significant number of schools; this was most com-

monly reported in girls' secondary schools while principals in vocational schools were least likely to see the programme as successful in this respect (Figure 6.4). In addition, Transition Year was seen as more successful in reducing drop-out in larger than in smaller schools (Table A6.2). Interestingly, schools with broader Transition Year programmes tended to see Transition Year as more positive in reducing student drop-out; 49 per cent of schools providing 8 or more subject areas felt that the programme was "very successful" in reducing drop-out compared with 32 per cent of those in schools providing fewer than five subject areas.

Similar findings were evident among teachers in the case-study schools with just over half deeming Transition Year to have been either very successful or successful in the reduction of school drop-out. Teachers in Victoria St. were somewhat more likely than those in other schools to view the programme as being very successful in this respect.

Figure 6.4: Perceived success of Transition Year in reducing drop-out from school (% of principals regarding it as "very successful")

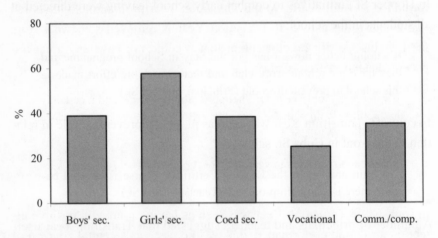

Source: Survey of School Principals (2001).

Three of the case-study schools (Hopper St., Cuba St. and Manners Mall) experienced some difficulties in student retention at senior cycle:

> Interviewer: At what stage do they tend to leave, would it be during Transition Year, in fifth year or across the board?

> Principal: It's across the board. Certainly, going into fourth year or going into fifth year and even in sixth year [we're] losing a few people who just say: I can't do this any more (Cuba St. school).

> We would have a fairly high retention rate up to Junior Cert and then the school would be bending over backwards to hold on to kids, which would be difficult in all sorts of ways. After that it's a real issue as to how we hold on to kids (Principal, Hopper St.).

The interviews highlighted the problems associated with the provision of Transition Year in an environment of relatively high drop-out at senior cycle level. In Cuba St., the principal found that Transition Year was only "somewhat successful" in reducing drop-out from school while in Hopper St., Transition Year was not seen as a particular factor in early school leaving:

> The school has a problem regarding drop-out. Some would blame Transition Year but I don't (Teacher, Hopper St.).

In Hopper St., initiatives to combat early school leaving were directed at all students in the school:

> It's doing better now, it has got the Stay in School programme and they have got a homework club and there was a big effort made in this school to prevent drop-out (Principal, Hopper St.).

In contrast, Transition Year was seen as playing a preventive role in relation to drop-out in Cuba St. school:

> A certain amount of the Leaving Certificate course is covered because there is a high drop-out rate (Teacher, Cuba St.).

A number of principals and teachers suggested that Transition Year itself may play a role in facilitating early school leaving. The Principal in Hopper St. felt that, while Transition Year was a positive influence overall, it had the potential to "seduce" some students out of the system given the extra time in school involved:

> It left too many gaps it seemed to them for people to fall through the mesh in terms of structure . . . But I think people went through Transition Year and in a way by the time they got to fifth year they were

seduced out of the system. Sometimes they would not have lasted anyway (Principal, Hopper St.).

While the principal of Willis St. felt that students are generally positive towards Transition Year, the uptake of part-time work was seen as causing a problem in terms of attendance and longer term retention among less academically inclined students:

> In the last couple of years now . . . we have lost a few, we have lost some students in TY and in fifth year. Again we are talking about the less academically driven students. Because there have been jobs on stream — now in some cases they got apprenticeships . . . which is fine, you know. They are moving, they are getting somewhere. But you would be a bit concerned where a lad gets some little dead end job that gives him money for fags and . . . maybe he comes back into fifth year and then he eventually disappears on you. There aren't any great prospects in the job (Principal, Willis St.).

In general, while a significant minority of principals see Transition Year as helping to reduce drop-out, staff in more disadvantaged schools highlighted the possible negative consequences of Transition Year participation for early school leaving.

6.1.4 Guidance in terms of subject choice and long-term career choice

The majority of principals surveyed considered increasing awareness of subject and career choices as very successful components of the Transition Year programme. There was little variation across types of schools in the perceived success of these aspects of the programme. However, principals in schools with broader Transition Year programmes tended to report greater success in promoting subject and career awareness (see Figure 6.5).

Figure 6.5: Perceived success of the Transition Year programme in promoting subject and career awareness by breadth of programme provision

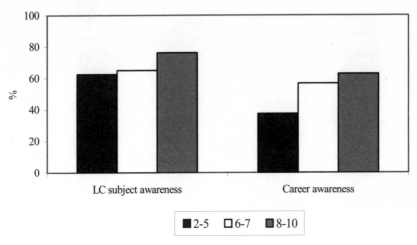

Source: Survey of School Principals (2001).

Within the case-study schools, a number of staff outlined the importance of the guidance provided by taking part in Transition Year, particularly in terms of the opportunity to try out different subjects:

> It's a chance for them to try some subjects they haven't taken before (Teacher, Wallace St.).

> It maybe gives the opportunity for a taste for a subject . . . maybe then choosing their subjects in fifth year, . . . they might choose . . . based on what they have done in TY rather than what they might have chosen in third year (Transition Year Co-ordinator, Victoria St.).

> But the actual Transition Year experience itself for them and the exposure they get to the various subjects, it gives them a fairly good grounding. Very few arrive [in fifth year] completely stuck and gobsmacked. Most of them are in fact quite focused and have a fair idea what they want (Guidance Counsellor, Wallace St.).

This was seen as particularly important for those students who were unsure about their intended educational and career pathway at the end of their Junior Cert year:

> Transition Year is very successful for students who are unsure of what they want from the Leaving Certificate. TY is not very academic, so it gives them a chance to explore new skills and subjects (Teacher, Wallace St.).

> They [the students] are thinking of where they are going at that stage. They have a class period in career guidance in TY as well. They are sort of being focused, thinking about careers, about subject choices, what they would need for a particular career (Principal, Willis St.).

The chance for students to make better-informed choices about their Leaving Certificate subjects was seen to have positive benefits in academic terms:

> It's too important to get the right subjects. If they're comfortable with the subjects, then I'm happy and there's no problems and they work and they study and their future opens up because they are obviously going to do better knowing that the subjects they have chosen are ones that they are happy and comfortable with (Guidance Counsellor, Mount Cook).

Teachers were asked if taking Transition Year has a specific impact on the kinds of subjects and careers that students choose afterwards. One guidance counsellor felt that it had a definite influence:

> I think in the area of the sciences it would because they would have had more exposure. Generally, I think it does and it gives them time to study themselves and see what subjects they actually want. I think coming into third year they are focusing on Junior Cert and usually they are very focused on the subjects and that may not be the best. I think they really do need a bit of time that Transition Year gives them (Guidance Counsellor, Victoria St.).

However, another guidance counsellor considered student choices to be quite fluid, even after taking Transition Year:

> I don't think it has a major influence, [in] some cases it will but in a lot of cases it won't. The percentage of students in sixth year that would actually label themselves before they go to college, know exactly what they want — physiotherapy, law or whatever, it is only about 20 to 25 per cent. The majority don't know (Guidance Counsellor, Mount Cook).

This section has explored the perceived success of particular aspects of the Transition Year programme. Generally, management and teachers see Transition Year as particularly successful in promoting personal and social development among students. It is also seen to have benefits in terms of promoting awareness of subject choices and career opportunities. However, a note of caution was sounded in terms of the potential negative effects of Transition Year on academic performance and school drop-out among some students. While this section has focused on the potential effects of Transition Year on students, the following section examines the extent to which the programme was seen as influencing teachers' own experiences of school life.

6.2 "WHAT'S IN IT FOR THE TEACHERS?"

In general, various aspects of the Transition Year programme were seen as positive by both management and teachers:

> Overall, I think it is a positive educational experience. It's an opportunity to go beyond the classroom and to identify and develop personal interests (Principal, Mt. Cook).

> The teachers approve TY, as far I know, I think they are pro TY. Nobody has said they wanted to see TY dropped and people have said that they wanted it kept on. So I would myself think that the majority of teachers want TY (Principal, Manners Mall).

Furthermore, only a very small number of the teachers surveyed in the case-study schools stated that they wanted the programme dropped from their schools (see Chapter Two).

Teachers were asked whether they felt that Transition Year was seen in a positive way by all teachers in their school. Forty-two per cent considered that Transition Year was seen positively by almost all teachers with a further forty per cent reporting it was seen as positive by more than half of the teaching staff. There was significant variation across the case-study schools in the responses to this question. Views about teacher perceptions were most positive in Victoria St., Manners Mall and Wallace St. with the most negative views evident in Cuba St.

As well as having an impact on students (see above), two aspects of the programme were seen as enhancing the professional lives of teachers themselves. The first aspect related to the opportunity for co-ordinators and teachers to engage in curriculum planning and design:

> The TYC brought his interests and enthusiasms to the subject and Transition Year was an opportunity for him to bring those interests into the educational system. Again, I would say that is a common experience (Principal, Mt. Cook).

> I think it gives teachers, if I can use the buzz-word, it empowered teachers as well to come up with curricula and change (Principal, Victoria St.).

Time was seen as a major factor in enhancing teacher opportunity to pursue certain professional interests. This was seen to be beneficial for both students and teachers:

> There's more activity, more time to raise and explore things that you don't get to do with an exam syllabus (Teacher, Manners Mall).

> We're not bounded by course exams. I can do things that I like and the pupils will pick up on that. That's the biggest advantage of Transition Year. In Leaving Certificate there's no room for other activities (Teacher, Wallace St.).

> I feel freer, not that constrained by syllabus, [we have] more time to discuss, follow something up (Teacher, Wallace St.).

> There's a lot more freedom, students can relax and enjoy themselves a bit more. We can cover topics but we don't have to cover them either. I enjoy it because I want to pass on my experience (Teacher, Victoria St.).

> There's more time, we're less pressurised and more relaxed (Teacher, Cuba St.).

However, in some contexts, lack of support and training were seen as causing difficulties in teachers' benefiting from their involvement in Transition Year (see also Chapter Five):

> Sometimes . . . teachers are coming back to me saying "I'm not skilled or trained" and I think there's a whole issue there in the sense that teachers are presumed to be skilled counsellors, are presumed to have a range of skills which are not available to them, which are not available to anybody at a certain level. . . . There is a whole set of expectations there about personal development issues . . . which are unrealistic (Principal, Hopper St.).

> I think it is a special course, it is not like fifth, it's not like first year, it's not even like repeat Leaving Cert. and it takes special skills and I think we are suffering from a skills shortage. I don't blame the teachers . . . because they continue to struggle with it but [we need] more input into things that they can do. It's really turning the teachers upside down, that's it (Principal, Cuba St.).

A second positive aspect, from the point of view of teachers, was the improved relationship between students and teachers as a result of Transition Year:

> They [students] tend to have better relationships with the teachers as a result of Transition Year which means that they are enjoying the subjects more and hence they do a little bit more work in the subjects (Transition Year Co-ordinator, Wallace St.).

> It gives them [students] an opportunity to do things they've never done before. It gives them an opportunity to see school and teachers in a different light (Teacher, Hopper St.).

> I think they also get a better relationship with the teachers because they are working with them rather than under them. I think there is a lot more co-operation (Transition Year Co-ordinator, Hopper St.).

In sum, as well as having benefits for students, Transition Year was also seen as having benefits for teachers themselves in allowing them to develop their professional interests and in improving the climate of the classroom. However, the extent to which Transition Year facilitated teachers' own development was seen as somewhat hindered by the lack of support and training for teachers, particularly in relation to personal development issues.

6.3 IS TRANSITION YEAR FOR EVERYONE?

Chapter Two has documented views within the case-study schools on whether the Transition Year programme should be compulsory or optional. In two of the schools where the programme was compulsory (or quasi-compulsory), the majority of teachers supported this approach while in the other two 'compulsory' schools teachers were more divided in their views. In schools where the programme is optional, teachers tend to support this approach; the exception to this pattern occurred in Victoria St. school where over half of teachers felt the programme should be compulsory for all students in their school (see Chapter Two).

Views about the appropriate form of Transition Year provision were echoed in teacher discussions of the benefits of the programme, with many teachers feeling that the programme benefits some students more than others:

> I think some students feel it is beneficial and some don't basically (Guidance Counsellor, Manners Mall).

The differential effects of Transition Year were seen to reflect a lack of interest on the part of some students:

> You always have a percentage of students who won't get involved. No matter how you lure them, they won't. Now I think they miss out. I think Transition Year is for students who want to get involved. You only get out of it what you put in and I'd say 85 to 90 per cent of students in this school put a lot in there and they get a lot out but there's always the 15 per cent who, for whatever reason, just aren't mature enough or haven't come to terms with themselves as a human being to make the step to contribute individually (Guidance Counsellor, Mt. Cook).

> A lot of students lack motivation. They're just not self-motivated. . . . I think that the programme is good, but they're afraid to stand out (Teacher, Wallace St.).

There are other students who really don't focus on it at all. It's the usual thing where you allow certain freedom and give them opportunities to meet deadlines and things like that. Not everybody can manage that and students find it very difficult to manage those sort of things and some of them slip back and lose interest . . . They all come in willingly but they all don't work at the same rate and they all don't benefit at the same rate (Principal, Wallace St.).

It was felt that some students become more lazy and undisciplined during Transition Year:

Transition Year does give a child time to stop off from their studies, to sample subjects and skills, and gives space for maturity. But they do tend to feel they're on holidays this year (Teacher, Manners Mall).

In theory it [TY] is to help them mature. It helps some but it doesn't help all. I don't know if they would have had the same progress if they didn't go on to Transition Year. It is damaging to see some students without commitment to study and school, without outside support. In Transition Year even the good students can drift out of habit (Teacher, Cuba St.).

It's very good on some students, some felt that they could do what they wanted. Some need discipline, but it doesn't suit every type of child (Teacher, Manners Mall).

These difficulties were sometimes placed in the context of a lack of structure within the programme itself:

The programme needs to become much more structured and it needs more substance. The value of TY needs to be looked at — it can be a bit of a time waster (Teacher, Hopper St.).

Teachers were asked about the proportion of students in their school who were positive about the programme. Twenty-eight per cent of teachers reported that "nearly all" students are positive with a further forty-seven per cent stating that "more than half" of students are positive about Transition Year. There is significant variation across schools in the responses: the most positive reports emerge from Victoria St., Mount Cook and Wallace St. with the most negative reports coming from Cuba St. Interestingly, although teachers in Manners Mall felt that the majority of teachers in the school were positive about Transition Year, they were less likely to see students as having positive perceptions. The extent to which teacher reports are consistent with students' own perceptions is discussed in Chapter Seven.

A similar question was asked of teachers concerning parental perceptions of Transition Year; 28 per cent reported that almost all parents of students in the school were positive about the programme with a further 45 per cent reporting that more than half of parents are positive. Again reported views varied significantly by school: views were seen as more positive in Victoria St., Mount Cook and Wallace St. with more negative views in Cuba St. and Hopper St.:

> I think there's a problem with parents and students in that they tend to undervalue something that doesn't have an exam and a certificate at the end of it. I don't think the average lay person can accurately assess the actual educational value of something unless you have got some piece of paper to wave at employers afterwards (Former TY co-ordinator, Hopper St.).

> Parents would have the anxiety that it was a doss year. "They don't have anything to do", all that kind of thing, which is wrong. But this is the perception (TY Co-ordinator, Cuba St. school).

In general, teachers, students and their parents were seen as positive about the Transition Year programme. However, teachers differed in the extent to which they saw the programme as suitable for all students. In particular, more motivated students were seen as getting more out of the year than other students.

6.4 SUGGESTIONS FOR CHANGES TO THE TRANSITION YEAR PROGRAMME

Management and teachers were asked about the main priorities for the future development of the Transition Year programme and about any potential improvements that could be made to the programme. A major recurring theme emerging from the interviews with teachers and school management was the need for the on-going adaptation and development of the programme from year to year. In a number of schools, on-going evaluation was used to assess the programme content:

> I suppose we have looked at Transition Years in other schools and seen things that they were doing and adapted things in and it is changed from experience. Whatever had worked well, we have kept and things that haven't worked well we have dropped. . . . I feel what we are doing now seems to have . . . settled fairly well and be very satisfactory (Principal, Manners Mall).

> Our programme has developed over the years on the basis of teachers with particular interests designing programmes, implementing them and then refining them (Principal, Mt. Cook).

> We do change it every year in the sense [that] if there is a new idea we try to incorporate it and I think we should continue to do so. I think it is very important that the review and the report is produced so that we have a point where we can say right this is where we are now and that review should also take into account anything for the future (Transition Year Co-ordinator, Mount Cook).

> The courses are quite flexible; some of them are historical . . . but most of the courses have evolved. . . . None of the courses have been stagnant. They have all evolved to a certain extent (Guidance Counsellor, Cuba St.).

Secondly, it was felt that the content of the programme should be student-led as well as student-centred:

> We don't give kids half enough credit for having ideas. They learn very quickly and they are testing the real world and that's what it's about. It's very important that we give them their head and let's see what they make of it because their ideas are fantastic (Guidance Counsellor, Mt. Cook).

> The Transition Year is more flexible. It depends on the class as well. You can have a class that are avid footballers and that's all they want to do. Obviously it's going to be a wider programme than that but you kind of cater to them somewhat (Transition Year Co-ordinator, Hopper St.).

However, some practical difficulties were envisaged with operationalis-
ing this approach:

> We have also tried to ask the incoming pupils when they are in third
> year what would they like but that's unrealistic because there is no
> reason why we should change our timetable every year just because
> the pupils are different. Often they don't know anyway, it's how the
> particular thing is taught (Transition Year Co-ordinator, Mount
> Cook).

Thirdly, staff felt that more trips and perhaps a greater focus on careers
activities should be incorporated into the programme:

> We should have a foreign trip and more national and international
> activities (Teacher, Hopper St.).

> With regard to the future, I think the vocational side of it has to come
> earlier and I think kids would respond to that because they want to
> know about their futures, they want a vision of themselves and some-
> times the educational system doesn't allow them that vision. It sort
> of clouds their future rather than opening it up. Students I think to-
> day, younger and younger, are becoming far more focused on what
> they want out of life (Guidance Counsellor, Mt. Cook).

> I'd like to be able to take them maybe . . . a little bit more into the
> career area, like for example the FÁS thing that went on in Dublin,
> the FÁS exhibition there at the beginning of the month would have
> been excellent exposure for them (Guidance Counsellor, Victoria
> St.).

Finally, finances were a major source of contention, with a number of
teachers highlighting the need for more funds to facilitate a more diverse
programme incorporating activities and outings:

> More funding is needed for extra trips. Transition Year should be
> funded as a stand-alone year and then it can be taken seriously
> (Teacher, Willis St.).

> We need Departmental funding for extra-curricular activities, such as
> going to dramas and plays. At the moment, they [students] have to
> pay for activities (Teacher, Hopper St.).

> We need more involvement with the wider community and the local facilities. We could spend more time outside, but it does create other problems, such as funding and transport (Teacher, Cuba St.).

> We need more funding for trips, then Transition Year would be more activity-based and fun (Teacher, Cuba St.).

Other issues highlighted included the need for more in-service training and for more classroom resources (see Chapter Five).

6.5 CONCLUSIONS

On the whole, school management and teachers were positive about various aspects of the Transition Year programme, most particularly with its impact on the personal and social development of students. However, principals in boys' secondary, vocational, small and/or designated disadvantaged schools were somewhat less likely to view the programme as successful as were those in schools with a compulsory Transition Year. Variation was also evident among the case-study schools with the most positive views of the programme reported in Victoria St. school, a pattern which relates to the level of staff involvement, co-operation among staff along with good teacher-student relations. Although there was a strong commitment to maintaining the Transition Year programme as compulsory in two of the case-study schools, a number of teachers across all schools felt that the programme was "not for everyone" and that the benefits accrued to those students who participated most actively in the year. The main suggestions for improving the programme centred on the need for on-going evaluation and development of programme content, having a more student-led focus, incorporating more trips and practical activities, enhanced funding, more access to in-service training and improved teaching resources.

APPENDIX A6.1: ADDITIONAL TABLES

Table A6.1: Perceived success of the programme by school type (% principals regarding it as "very successful")

Dimension	Boys' Sec.	Girls' Sec.	Coed-Sec.	Voc.	Comm./ Comp.	Sig.
Personal Development	94.9	99.0	90.3	94.2	97.8	NS
Social Skills	67.2	84.8	71.0	75.7	84.4	NS
Academic Performance	39.3	50.0	41.7	36.2	37.8	p<.05
Reducing Drop Out	38.9	58.0	37.9	25.4	37.5	p<.01
Guidance Re LC Subject Choice	63.3	72.2	71.0	65.7	80.4	NS
Guidance Re Long Term Career Choice	45.0	62.6	56.5	52.2	65.2	NS
Overall success score	*2.56*	*2.70*	*2.61*	*2.55*	*2.66*	*p<.01*
N	*63*	*105*	*64*	*64*	*39*	

Note: NS — not statistically significant.

Source: Survey of School Principals (2001).

Table A6.2: Perceived success of the programme by school size (% of principals regarding it as "very successful")

Dimension	<400	400-599	600+	Sig
Personal Development	92.5	97.1	97.3	NS
Social Skills	69.4	80.0	82.7	p<.05
Academic Performance	33.1	42.7	51.4	NS
Reducing Drop Out	33.6	34.7	57.0	p<.01
Guidance Re LC Subject Choice	69.2	68.3	72.5	NS
Guidance Re Long Term Career Choice	50.8	61.0	58.7	NS
Overall success score	*2.56*	*2.62*	*2.69*	*p<.001*
N	*123*	*109*	*103*	

Note: NS — not statistically significant·

Source: Survey of School Principals (2001).

Table A6.3: Perceived success of the programme by designated disadvantaged status (% of principals regarding it as "very successful")

Dimension	Disadvantaged	Not Disadvantaged	
Personal Development	94.3	95.6	NS
Social Skills	74.4	78.0	NS
Academic Performance	31.4	45.9	p<.05
Reducing Drop Out	31.7	44.7	NS
Guidance Re LC Subject Choice	63.5	72.2	NS
Guidance Re Long Term Career Choice	52.9	57.4	p<.05
Overall success score	*2.55*	*2.65*	*p<.01*
N	*83*	*252*	

Note: NS — not statistically significant.

Source: Survey of School Principals (2001).

Table A6.4: Perceived success of the programme by nature of provision (% of principals regarding it as "very successful")

Dimension	Compulsory	Optional	
Personal Development	91.3	96.9	p<.05
Social Skills	68.8	80.0	p<.05
Academic Performance	32.1	45.4	p<.001
Reducing Drop Out	33.3	43.8	NS
Guidance Re LC Subject Choice	69.1	70.6	NS
Guidance Re Long Term Career Choice	51.3	58.3	NS
Overall success score	*2.55*	*2.65*	*p<.01*
N	*80*	*254*	

Note: NS — not statistically significant.

Source: Survey of School Principals (2001).

Table A6.5: Overall success rating by timing of introduction of Transition Year

Timing of Introduction	Success Score
<6 years previously	2.57
>6 years previously	2.66
Significance	*p<.01*

Note: NS — not statistically significant.

Source: Survey of School Principals (2001).

Chapter Seven

STUDENTS' PERCEPTIONS OF TRANSITION YEAR

INTRODUCTION

This chapter draws on group interviews with students in the case-study schools to explore their perceptions of the Transition Year programme. While students in the midst of doing the programme will not be in a position to assess the longer term impact of taking Transition Year, their views will yield useful insights into the aspects of the programme that are more successful than others. The first section explores the nature of student-teacher interaction within Transition Year. The second section highlights what students see as positive aspects of the programme while the perceived negative aspects are discussed in section three. In section four, the issue of whether students feel they should have the choice to take, or not to take, the programme is discussed. Section five highlights the improvements to the programme suggested by students.

7.1 STUDENT–TEACHER RELATIONS WITHIN TRANSITION YEAR

One of the main themes highlighted in the student interviews was the way in which the nature of student-teacher interaction was different in Transition Year than at junior cycle level. Overall, students felt that teachers were more relaxed and friendly in Transition Year than in previous years:

> The teachers are more laid back with you . . . you are allowed do a lot more. The teachers aren't watching over you as much (Student, Cuba St.).

> They [the teachers] treat us with a bit more respect (Student, Mt. Cook).

> You get much more respect. Yes, you are treated more maturely (Student, Manners Mall).

> As a year group we got on with the teachers. A lot of them did put in extra time, things we did they put a lot of work into it (Student, Mt. Cook).

This change in student-teacher relations was seen as reflecting in part the students' own maturity:

> They respect you a lot more because you are older so if you have an opinion, they will hear you out. Before they would just shout at you. They wouldn't let you talk (Student, Wallace St.).

However, students saw the lack of exam pressure within Transition Year as a more important factor in improving the informal climate for their year group and for teachers:

> Interviewer: So do you think teachers treat you differently than they did last year?

> Student: A bit. You are more mature. It's not really that. Like last year you were pressured into work, it's the Junior Cert. You just hear a lot about the Junior Cert. It's like study, study, study and then when you get into this year there is not much to do (Student, Mt. Cook).

> We are more friendly with them. You find that as you go up, you are more friendly with the teachers. They are not working towards a goal either this year. They are not under pressure either. Because they were under pressure as well last year when we were doing exams because they had to get a certain course done. . . . So I suppose this year we are all more relaxed and the teachers are more on our level (Student, Higher band, Victoria St.).

> Teachers aren't as strict as they are in other years really because there is no pressure (Student, Wallace St.).

Nonetheless, the lack of exam pressure was not always seen as a positive aspect of the programme (see section 7.3 below). Students often perceived the lack of exam pressure in a negative light, especially when talking about the consequences for teachers:

> I think that the teachers are using it as a doss. I think it's a doss for them as well as us (Student, Lower band, Willis St.).

> Some of the classes that we do . . . are boring this year because the teachers . . . don't really get us to do much because there is no pressure on them to get results out of us so they let us kind of do what we want (Student, Wallace St.).

> They [the teachers] are not that bothered because they don't think it is an important year (Student, Lower band, Victoria St.).

> They just leave you. They don't put any pressure on you to learn at all. Earlier on I said that [I did] this year because I didn't want any pressure. But you kind of need a bit of pressure in a year to get you motivated and learn all the stuff whereas this year you say "yes, I will do it in a minute" (Student, Wallace St.).

A number of students reported that Transition Year had led to improved interaction with *some* rather than all teachers:

> You get to know some of the teachers a bit better, the ones that want to get to know you better. They all try to talk to you where there are other ones who wouldn't bother (Student, Wallace St.).

Some of the students in Cuba St., for example, perceived their relationship to be better with younger teachers rather than with longer established staff:

> Some of the teachers who started this year are real nice. They are easier to get on with because they understand more where you are coming from and they actually like teaching. The teachers who have been here longer don't have any time for you. But the younger teachers talk to you and then you will talk back to them (Student, Cuba St.).

A contrasting situation was evident in Hopper St. where a number of students reported that teachers were more strict than they had been at junior cycle level. This seemed, at least in part, to reflect the greater emphasis on regular homework and formal exams within the Transition Year programme in Hopper St (see Chapter Five):

> I think they are more strict, some of the teachers we didn't have last year but they seem more strict than last year (Student, Lower band, Hopper St.).

> No, [the teachers don't ask us what we'd like to do] . . . you do what they tell you to do. The teachers were saying "did we give yis too much homework?" and all of us said "yeah" but it doesn't change anything (Student, Lower band, Hopper St.).

In general, with the exception of Hopper St. school, Transition Year was seen as facilitating improved relations between teachers and students, mainly because of the lack of exam pressure. However, some students reported that the lack of exam pressure meant that some teachers became less interested in classwork.

7.2 POSITIVE ASPECTS OF TRANSITION YEAR

Students tended to choose Transition Year because they felt it was a break from exam pressure, would give them an opportunity to take a different range of subjects, would give them time to explore career options and would contribute to their overall development and maturity (see Chapter Three). These themes were again evident when students discussed their views on the positive aspects of the Transition Year programme.

A number of students stressed the content of the Transition Year programme. Firstly, they felt that the programme gave them access to subjects that they otherwise would not have had the chance to try:

> We had more variety of subjects which you wouldn't have had a chance to do, like journalism (Student, Cuba St.).

> It's good changing [subjects] because you get to sample everything. You don't get too bored doing the same thing every day (Student, Cuba St.).

> I found it interesting because I get to do subjects that I wouldn't ac-
> tually do if I were in Junior Cert or Leaving Cert. I wouldn't do them
> for an exam because I'm not good at them (Student, Wallace St.).

Secondly, work experience was seen as a useful component of Transition
Year in terms of future career planning:[11]

> I mean the work experience would be better as well. It would give
> you a better idea of what you actually wanted to do when you leave
> school (Student, Cuba St.).

> Interviewer: And somebody mentioned that before you went into
> Transition Year, you weren't sure what you wanted to do?

> Student: I had an idea but if I got nothing out of Transition Year at
> all at least I got one thing. It's that I know what I want to do when I
> leave and I am more positive when I leave school (Student, Lower
> band, Victoria St.).

> It matures you more regarding subject choices and career because
> you talk to different people about different choices and careers. You
> go and talk to people about different choices and different careers.
> Loads of people change their minds over the year, because they're so
> into it (Student, Mt. Cook).

Thirdly, a lot of students emphasised trips and activities as the most positive aspect of Transition Year:

> The group really comes together when you go away on trips. It's just
> a really good laugh. Everyone has a really good time (Student, Mt.
> Cook).

> There are plenty of trips. There is a lot more experience. I thought it
> would be duller than it is but it is better actually (Student, Lower
> band, Willis St.).

Fourthly, the approach to learning and in particular the emphasis on project-work was seen as an advantage of the programme:

---

[11] However, it should be noted that students differed in the extent to which they used
their work experience placements to sample career options (see Chapter Four).

I had heard "oh, Transition Year is a doss", but you do more practical work like projects and stuff. I didn't expect to be doing so much of that. You are a lot more tired this year than you were in Junior Cert because you are doing so much. You don't really realise it yourself but looking back you realise you have done loads (Student, Higher band, Victoria St.).

It's a different sort of pressure to that of the Leaving Certificate. You have to learn things and the project work is more like research and then learning (Student, Cuba St.).

In Mount Cook school in particular (see Chapter Five), Transition Year was seen as allowing students to have an input into the content of courses:

They give you a choice of what you would like to do as against just doing what they like to do (Student, Mount Cook).

As they had anticipated, a number of students felt that Transition Year gave them a break from examination pressure:

I like it because it does give you a break from everything, from studying all the time and everything and it takes the pressure off you (Student, Cuba St.).

There is not as much pressure. You don't have exams. You don't feel I have to do something for the exams. You can take your time, you are not rushing to get it ready for the exams (Student, Lower band, Willis St.).

It was a break after the two years; it gives you a break after doing the Junior Cert (Student, Cuba St.).

We get enough [homework] but there's not a lot of pressure like there used to be in other years. It's a lot more easygoing but there is work involved (Student, Lower band, Willis St.).

Interviewer: Now would you have done Transition Year from the beginning by choice?

Student: No, I would have skipped it to get out of school quicker, to finish school quicker. But now like I'm glad that I did it. Yeah, it was a break after the two years; it gives you a break after doing the Junior Cert (Cuba St.).

Finally, a number of students (particularly those in Victoria St.) felt that the year had made them more mature and better integrated into the school:

> I like the way you get to know a lot of people that you wouldn't otherwise because our class has become really close now because we are together all the time (Student, Lower band, Victoria St.).

> You get the chance to know yourself as well. It sounds stupid but you get to know what you like and what you are best at and what you are not good at (Student, Lower band, Victoria St.).

> I look back now and think about it we did a good amount of stuff and I did enjoy myself because I got to know loads more girls, make loads of friends and have fun. The best memories I would have of all the school probably would be TY anyway (Student, Lower band, Victoria St.).

Increased maturity was also seen as having positive benefits for entry to the Leaving Cert programme:

> Transition Year has got me looking ahead now so I know what I want and I know how I'm going to do it and I am ready for it because last year it was "Oh God, fifth year is going to jump on me now if I don't do Transition Year" (Student, Higher band, Victoria St.).

> It kind of makes you more mature. And I find now I am looking forward to just getting back into the work because I am just a bit bored. . . . So I think that next year and the year after I will do more and hopefully I will get my points (Student, Mt. Cook).

> You have matured a lot. Some people would say we have gone backwards. But really we have matured even if we don't know it and we know we have to work [in fifth year] (Student, Higher band, Victoria St.).

In sum, students emphasised a number of positive aspects of Transition Year, including the chance to take different subjects, the work experience placement(s), trips and activities, and a different approach to learning. In addition, Transition Year was seen as providing a break from exam pressure and a chance for students to mature.

7.3 Negative Aspects of Transition Year

While many students emphasised positive aspects of the Transition Year programme, some students mentioned particular problems with the programme while a group of students had negative perceptions of the value of the programme overall. The latter group emphasised that Transition Year was "a waste of time", "boring" and a "doss":

> Student: We were foolish [to decide to do Transition Year].
>
> Interviewer: Why do you say that?
>
> Student: Because it's a waste of time (Student, Lower band, Willis St.).
>
> You sometimes think it's nice to have a doss. It's nice to have a doss the odd time but not for five days a week (Students, Lower band, Willis St.).
>
> Well, I expected a doss and I got it (Student, Cuba St.).

A number of aspects of the programme were emphasised by students. Firstly, some students felt that little "work" was done in Transition Year and that this would mean greater difficulties for them on entering fifth year:

> It's a doss year; you do nothing at all. You do [some work] in some schools, but you don't do as much as you would in second and third years. You are left behind [in terms of the school work]. I wouldn't do it again if I had the choice (Student, Cuba St.).
>
> It makes you wasters because you are doing nothing (Student, Lower band, Willis St.).
>
> We thought it would have been a lot more interesting. To be honest with you it's kind of boring. I thought we would have learned more. We actually haven't learned anything this year (Student, Wallace St.).
>
> Student: I don't know why you should relax in fourth year because when you go into fifth year after fourth year and you will fall behind. You will be useless.
>
> Interviewer: Some people think it might be good to have a break after their Junior Cert?

> Student: Yes, for some of us it is grand but it would be better to keep yourself going, to keep yourself into it, to get it over and done with fast when everything is in your head instead of a year of doing nothing, nothing compared to the Junior Cert (Student, Lower band, Willis St.).

> In class we do a good bit but we don't seem to get a lot of homework and sometimes it's a waste (Student, Mt. Cook).

Even where students were broadly positive about the programme, they expressed some concern about starting on the Leaving Certificate programme:

> Last year I used to know that I would give an hour to study each night and I had a routine. But this year it's really hard to get into a routine and I wouldn't really want to because you just take it as it comes and there is not much pressure for studying. It's more relaxed so I think it will be really hard to get back into a study routine. I am not looking forward to that but I suppose once you get into it, it will be fine (Student, Higher band, Victoria St.).

> I'm dreading going back into fifth year, all the study and all the homework. I think I will just die when I go in there (Student, Lower band, Victoria St.).

The exception to this pattern occurred in Hopper St., where students felt that there was an over-emphasis on homework and examinations within the Transition Year programme:

> We had to do Christmas tests. We are not supposed to get all these Christmas tests at all and we are getting them (Student, Lower band, Hopper St.).

> Interviewer: And has it turned out what you expected from what you heard?

> Student: [TY is] harder. You actually do work. Last year they didn't really seem to do any tests or anything and this year you have to do projects (Student, Higher band, Hopper St.).

Secondly, a number of students emphasised the content of the programme in their particular school, in particular a lack of variety in the
courses offered and the absence of activities and trips:

> I thought it would be a lot more interesting and more things to do
> (Student, Mount Cook).

> Every year they [TY students] were offered trips and we just got
> nothing. We weren't offered anything (Student, Mt. Cook).

> Student: We haven't been on any trips this year. We were promised
> we would go on load of trips.

> Interviewer: Have you not gone on any trips?

> Student: No, we went on a hill walk. We did more trips in third year
> at this stage by this time of the year (Lower band students, Hopper
> St.).

> I expected a few projects. I thought we could do more field work. I
> thought we would have taken more trips (Student, Mt. Cook).

Thirdly, the financial costs involved in Transition Year participation
caused difficulties for some students. In Hopper St., students were concerned about having to pay for expensive books which they felt were not
necessary:

> First student: There was a book on ECDL [European Computer
> Drivers' Licence]. . . . That was £25, and we never use it.

> Second student: No, we use it, but we won't be using it for long. But
> you had to buy it.

> Third student: If you didn't, you weren't allowed in the class (Stu-
> dents, Lower band, Hopper St.).

Students in Willis St. did not expect to have to pay so much in Transition
Year for school trips and guest speakers:

> [We should] do more activities like and more trips and [they should]
> subsidise some of the money. They cost so much money. You are
> paying out a fierce amount. The worst thing about Transition Year is
> really the money. I mean we spent more money this year than any

> other year. Yet we don't need any books for the year (Student,
> Higher band, Willis St.).

> It's not really the trips, about five euro for the bus or whatever. But
> for people coming in like the law day you had to pay for that. That
> was ten euro (Student, Higher band, Willis St.).

Students also felt concerned about the consequent financial pressure on
their parents:

> You have all the set days. You feel sorry when you don't want to go
> asking your parents every week if you could have money for this.
> I'm sure they would give it to you but you feel here I am asking
> them again (Student, Higher band, Victoria St.).

Three of the case-study schools grouped students by ability into Transition Year classes. It is interesting to note that in two of the three schools
(Hopper St. and Willis St.), perceptions of the programme were more
negative among students in the lower ability band than among those in
the higher ability band. In both of these schools, participation in Transition Year was compulsory or quasi-compulsory. In contrast, in Victoria
St. School, which had a high level of voluntary participation in the programme, broadly positive views of Transition Year were evident among
both higher and lower band students. It may be that, where some participants are unwilling, the concentration of less academic students in particular classes fosters a more negative climate for the operation of the
programme.

As well as variation within schools, there were differences between
schools in student perceptions of Transition Year with a significant
group of students expressing negative views of the programme in Cuba
St., Manners Mall and Hopper St. schools, all schools with greater con-
centrations of working-class students, and the most positive perceptions
of Transition Year found among students in Victoria St. school, a school
which was mixed in intake but had a strong orientation to third-level
education.

7.4 TRANSITION YEAR: IS IT FOR EVERYONE?

Students were asked about whether they felt that Transition Year should be compulsory or optional for students and whether they would recommend other students to take the programme. The pattern of responses echoed students' overall perceptions of the Transition Year. However, while many students in schools where Transition Year was compulsory were glad that they had taken the programme, almost all students emphasised that a choice should be given regarding participation. In contrast, two students in Mount Cook mentioned the logistical problems this might create in some contexts:

> First student: I think it would be really difficult if it's an option within school if half of your friends went on.

> Second student: I think if only half the year did it we wouldn't have enough people to do anything so I am glad everyone in our school had to do it (Mount Cook school).

Many students stressed that the programme was not "for everyone", with greater benefits accruing to those who actively participated in the programme:

> I would say you make of it what you put into it. If you put your work into it you will enjoy it (Student, Cuba St.).

> I think it's totally up to yourself as well what you put into it. If you do your homework every night. If you put effort into those projects and if you take on extra hobbies and if you do other things that you have time for now, then it's definitely worth it. But if you go along like you have been going along the whole time and you don't put anything extra into this year, then you probably wouldn't get that much enjoyment. You get out as much as you put into it (Student, Higher band, Victoria St.).

> They would have to do the work because it is worth it. Because you would be bored if you don't (Student, Wallace St.).

In addition, it was felt that less academically motivated students might not benefit from the programme to the same extent:

> For somebody who is pure lazy and extremely laid-back, I wouldn't advise them to do it because it would be very hard for them to get back into fifth year (Student, Lower band, Victoria St.).

> If they want to finish school early, if they have some plans after school and they know what they want to do [they shouldn't do TY] (Student, Cuba St.).

However, students also stressed that the success of Transition Year was contingent on how it operated within the particular school:

> It would depend on what the school was like. . . . I think we are lucky. I think our Transition Year programme is a lot better than some other schools' programmes. . . . I know people who find Transition Year great but in other schools they think it's a complete waste of time. It depends on the person a lot (Student, Mt. Cook).

> It depends on what the school offers (Student, Lower band, Hopper St.).

> First student: I would say look and see how the school does it first and decide.

> Second student: Yes, it does need to be well organised.

> Third student: You hear people talking about schools and fourth year — what they do here is pretty good and you are kept busy for the majority of the time but you will find in other schools they are actually quite bored. They don't do a lot with them. The teachers have the attitude that well third year and sixth year are more important. You just sit there and do whatever (Mt. Cook school).

> It seems in other schools you have options in your classes. In this school you are told in your class what you have to do. I wouldn't recommend it in this school (Student, Manners Mall).

In sum, students generally felt Transition Year participation should be a matter of choice. Many students stressed that the programme was more suitable for more motivated students and its success depended on how well a programme was run in a particular school.

7.5 SUGGESTIONS FOR IMPROVING TRANSITION YEAR

Students were asked whether they could suggest any potential improvements to the Transition Year programme. The main suggestion offered by students centred on the need to incorporate more trips and practical activities into the programme:

> I'd say put more activities into it, like more outings, not just go to places like FÁS. That is sort of putting pressure on you. So I would say more activities and more outings (Student, Manners Mall).

> More activities, more field work and more choice of classes. More interesting projects, things that you write out. For instance a fashion show — something that would be interesting, people would be interested in, not writing out a report for something. That really isn't interesting (Students, Mt. Cook).

> I think you could make a requirement and say that you had to take them somewhere. There should be things in place where schools could actually go on trips. They should have centres (Student, Mt. Cook).

> Like a foreign trip — for French students to go to France or Spanish students to go to Spain and so on. That would be helpful. And it's the perfect time in fourth year because you don't do much else (Student, Mt. Cook).

Some students emphasised the need for a greater variety of courses within the year:

> Student: [They should] get more teachers to do more subjects.

> Interviewer: Are there any subjects that you can think of that you would like to do?

> Student: Woodwork (Wallace St. school).

> There should be choices — that's about it (Student, Manners Mall).

Other students thought that the programme itself should become more structured:

> First student: A bit more of a syllabus maybe. There should be more research into books that could be brought out for fourth years or

something and maybe even in languages there should be more research done.

Second student: There should be a structure or maybe a general syllabus where maybe you would pick certain things to do.

Third student: It's hard for a school to have such a broad range as well for them to work in. Text-books would be a good idea (Student, Mount Cook).

Say you did ten classes, five classes should be fun and have interesting stuff and for the core subjects they should make you do work (Student, Wallace St.).

Another suggestion related to the need for greater co-operation and contact between schools and students doing Transition Year:

If there were more things where people were interacting. Maybe not even in this area, maybe the other end of the country where they get to know the people from [other schools]. If they had workshops or something like, with different schools. You could do swap-overs for a couple of days. It would be an experience. You could relate it into different topics (Students, Mt. Cook).

In sum, suggestions for improvement included having more trips and practical activities, a greater variety of courses and a more structured programme.

7.6 CONCLUSIONS

Students interviewed for the study felt that the Transition Year programme had a number of benefits, including the chance to try different subjects and activities, the opportunity to take part in work experience, and improved relations with teachers. However, a number of students were critical of the programme in terms of its lack of interest and the financial costs involved. Even where students were positive about the programme, many anticipated problems in settling back into the Leaving Certificate programme.

Variation was evident between the case-study schools in student perceptions of Transition Year. As with the teachers (see Chapter Six), the most positive views were expressed by students in Victoria St. Differences between schools in student perceptions tended to reflect the presence of a diverse programme, trips and practical activities, and good relations with teachers. However, these were not sufficient conditions since in many schools students were divided between those who enjoyed the programme and those who did not. The most negative perceptions were apparent among students in schools where Transition Year was compulsory *and* they were grouped into lower ability classes. Being obliged to take part in Transition Year therefore seems to fuel student disaffection if students with less positive orientations to school are concentrated in particular class groups. Almost all students interviewed felt that Transition Year should be optional and suggested improvements centred on more trips and practical activities along with a more diverse programme.

Chapter Eight

TRANSITION YEAR PARTICIPATION AND STUDENT OUTCOMES

INTRODUCTION

Chapters Six and Seven have explored perceptions of the Transition Year programme among school management, Transition Year co-ordinators, teachers and students. While these perceptions provide a useful insight into the nature of the programme, they do not allow us to assess the actual impact of Transition Year participation on student outcomes. This chapter sets out to examine the differences between Transition Year participants and non-participants in terms of a range of outcomes, including school drop-out, Leaving Certificate subject take-up and performance, entry to higher education, course choice within higher education, and early labour market careers. Chapter Two has indicated that students who take Transition Year tend to have more highly educated parents, more positive attitudes to school life and higher educational aspirations. It is therefore important to take account of these initial differences between participants and non-participants in looking at the impact of Transition Year.

8.1 SCHOOL DROPOUT

The Schools Database allows us to identify Transition Year students only if they have stayed in school until the Leaving Certificate exam (see Chapter One). We are, therefore, unable to determine whether students who have taken part in the Transition Year programme have different dropout patterns from non-participants over the senior cycle. However, it is possible to analyse differences in dropout patterns between schools with compulsory, optional or no Transition Year programme, controlling for differences between these schools in the nature of their student intake.

Figure 8.1 presents the raw dropout rates by type of Transition Year provision, distinguishing between students from different social class backgrounds. As might be expected from previous research (see, for example, Smyth and Hannan, 2000), students from working-class backgrounds have significantly higher dropout rates than other students. Among those from professional backgrounds, there is little variation in patterns of early school leaving by the nature of Transition Year provision. However, among students from semi-skilled or unskilled manual backgrounds, dropout rates are higher in schools where Transition Year is compulsory (35 per cent) than where the programme is optional (25 per cent) or not provided at all (24 per cent).

Figure 8.1: Senior cycle dropout by Transition Year provision and parental social class

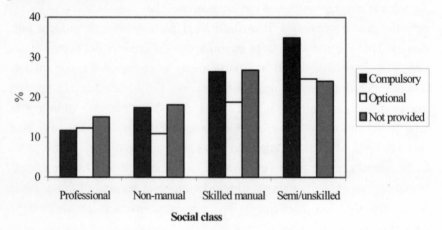

Source: The Schools Database.

Multivariate analyses were conducted to see if these differences by type of Transition Year provision were due to other differences in student intake. Multilevel modelling techniques were used to take account of the fact that students within a particular school are likely to resemble each other in certain key respects (see Chapter One). Because the outcome is dichotomous (leaving school before the Leaving Cert or not), a multilevel logistic model is used. Positive coefficients indicate the particular factor is associated with increased chances of school dropout while negative coefficients indicate reduced chances of early school leaving. The definitions of the variables used are presented in Appendix 8.1.

Senior cycle dropout rates are found to be higher among males than females but there are no net differences in dropout rates between schools by (type of) Transition Year programme (see Table 8.1, Model 1). Older students and those with lower Junior Cert grades are much more likely to drop out of school than other students. However, the effects of parental background are mainly mediated by student performance; that is, students from middle-class backgrounds are less likely to drop out of school than working-class students primarily because they experience greater success within the examination system (Model 2). When family background and prior performance are taken into account, schools with compulsory Transition Year programmes are found to have a dropout rate 1.4 times higher than other school types (Table 8.1, Model 2). In other words, schools with compulsory Transition Year programmes do not have greater dropout overall but have higher dropout rates than might be expected given their student profile. The differences in dropout rates between schools with compulsory or optional programmes and those without a Transition Year programme are presented in Figure 8.2. The first set of columns indicates overall differences, the second set shows differences controlling for student background and performance while the third set of columns indicates differences controlling for background, performance and student attitudes prior to the Junior Cert exam.

Figure 8.2: Dropout patterns by type of Transition Year provision (Odds ratios compared with schools not providing Transition Year)

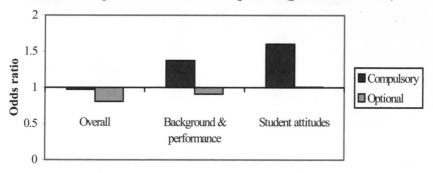

Note: Derived from the models in Table 8.1.

Table 8.1: Student dropout and Transition Year provision (Multilevel logistic regression based on 5,417 students in 108 schools)

	Model 1	Model 2	Model 3
Constant	−1.198	−2.000	−1.294
Female	−0.646*	−0.385*	−0.110
(Ref.: Male)			
TY provision:			
Compulsory	−0.026	0.317**	0.472*
Optional	−0.214	−0.095	−0.009
(Ref.: TY not provided)			
Family background:			
Higher professional		0.016	0.038
Lower professional		0.007	0.036
Other non-manual		−0.387*	−0.407*
Skilled manual		−0.042	−0.045
(Ref.: Semi/unskilled manual)			
Parents Third level		0.028	0.113
(Ref.: Other education)			
Age		0.495*	0.489*
Ability test score		0.006	0.008
Junior Cert performance		−0.730*	−0.579*
Student attitudes:			
Academic self-image			−0.058
Positive interaction			0.131
Negative interaction			0.134
School satisfaction			−0.111*
School recreation			0.017
Low attendance			0.665*
(Ref.: Average/good attendance)			
Vocational subjects			0.101
Unclear occupational aspirations			−0.166
(Ref.: Specified occup. aspiration)			
Aspire to Leaving Cert			−1.218*
Aspire to Certificate			−1.507*
Aspire to Degree			−1.084*
(Ref.: Aspire to Junior Cert)			
School-level variance	0.506*	0.235*	0.205*

Note: * $p < .05$, ** $p < .10$.

Source: The Schools Database.

Dropout patterns are also found to relate to differences between students in their attitudes to school in third year. Students who are broadly satisfied with school life are less likely to drop out of school (Table 8.1, Model 3). In keeping with previous research (see, for example, Smyth, 1999), school dropout is preceded by recurrent absenteeism with greater school retention found among students with good attendance records. As might be expected, educational aspirations in third year are highly predictive of subsequent educational participation (Table 8.1, Model 3). Even controlling for student attitudes and background, students with lower Junior Cert exam grades are much more likely to drop out of school before the Leaving Cert than those with higher grades. Controlling for student attitudes, schools with a compulsory Transition Year programme continue to have higher drop-out rates than other school types (see also Figure 8.2).

Additional analyses were conducted to explore whether the impact of Transition Year provision varied by social class background, as Figure 8.1 had indicated might be the case. Drop-out rates were found to be higher in schools with compulsory Transition Year among all groups except for students from professional backgrounds (analyses not shown here). However, this variation by social class was no longer significant when prior ability/performance and student attitudes to school were taken into account.

8.2 SUBJECT TAKE-UP AT LEAVING CERTIFICATE LEVEL

Chapter Four has indicated that schools differ in the kinds of subjects they provide within Transition Year. The exposure to different subjects as part of the Transition Year programme may have an effect on the type of subjects students subsequently take for the Leaving Cert. Analyses were conducted for selected subjects: whether students took one or more science subjects, one or more business subjects, French, History, Geography, and one or more vocational subjects. While subject take-up is shaped by a complex interaction between school provision, informal school climate and student "choice" (see Smyth and Hannan, 2002), even a simple model of subject take-up may yield some insight into the potential differences between Transition Year participants and non-participants in the subjects they take at Leaving Cert level.

All else being equal, subject take-up at Leaving Cert level is significantly influenced by gender with vocational subjects being predominantly male, and French being predominantly female, in profile. Business subjects and science are also predominantly female, although in the case of science, the pattern is driven by the high proportion of female students taking Biology. Take-up patterns also vary by family background characteristics with students from professional backgrounds over-represented in science subjects and under-represented in History. Subject take-up at Leaving Cert is strongly influenced by having taken the relevant subject at Junior Cert (see Appendix 8.1 for a definition of the relevant subjects). In addition, attitudes prior to the Junior Cert are highly predictive of subsequent subject take-up. Students with a preference for mathematical and scientific subjects are much more likely to take science subjects and much less likely to take History or Geography. In contrast, those who prefer subjects like English are much more likely to do History or business subjects and much less likely to take scientific subjects. Students who prefer practical subjects are more likely to take vocational subjects at Leaving Cert level and less likely to take History or French. In addition, higher-performing students (that is, those who achieved higher exam grades overall at Junior Cert) are over-represented in French and science subjects while lower-performing students are over-represented in Geography and vocational subjects.

The set of models in Table 8.2 allows us to explore the effect of Transition Year on subject choice controlling for gender, parental background, prior ability/performance, subject take-up at junior cycle and attitudes to subjects in third year. The impact of Transition Year is depicted in Figure 8.3. Transition Year students do not differ significantly from other students in their likelihood of taking a science subject or History for the Leaving Cert. However, all else being equal, students who have taken Transition Year are 1.4 times more likely to study Geography and only half as likely as other students to take a vocational subject for the Leaving Cert. The pattern for the take-up of vocational subjects may relate to the somewhat lower provision level of such subjects as part of the Transition Year programme (see Chapter Four). However, the pattern for Geography is somewhat surprising, given it is provided as part of fewer than half of Transition Year programmes. The pattern may relate, however, to the interdisciplinary nature of Geography since Transition Year students have frequently studied subjects which cross existing subject boundaries.

Table 8.2: Leaving Cert subject take-up and Transition Year participation (Multilevel logistic regression; 4,434 students in 108 schools)

	Science (1 or more)	Business (1 or more)	French	History	Geography	Vocational subject
Constant	-1.485	-1.426	-5.710	-1.329	-1.638	-3.085
Gender	0.792*	0.595*	1.560*	-0.261*	-0.200*	-2.554*
Took Transition Year	-0.048	0.573*	0.320**	0.030	0.346*	-0.505*
Took TY*female	-0.315	-0.790*	-0.541*	-0.048	-0.079	0.308
(Ref.: Did not take TY)						
Parental class:						
Higher professional	0.507*	-0.170	0.058	-0.458*	-0.052	0.140
Lower professional	0.329*	-0.157	0.035	-0.315*	0.040	0.149
Other non-manual	0.147	-0.167	0.422*	-0.423*	0.070	0.141
Skilled manual	0.095	-0.013	0.101	-0.425*	0.106	0.229
(Ref.: Semi/unskilled)						
Parental education:						
Third-level education	0.170	-0.095	0.024	-0.026	-0.060	-0.059
(Ref.: Other education)						

Ability test score	0.007**	-0.002	-0.008**	-0.001	-0.004	-0.001
Took relevant subject for Junior Cert (Ref.: Did not take)	1.889*	1.927*	6.101*	1.139*	1.362*	2.663*
Attitudes in third year:						
Maths/Science orientation	0.261*	-0.004	0.062	-0.175*	-0.086*	0.092
English orientation	-0.269*	0.145*	0.023	0.339*	0.029	-0.100
Vocational orientation	0.023	-0.164*	-0.130*	-0.396*	0.011	0.649*
Junior Cert performance	0.235*	-0.020	0.371*	-0.023	-0.160*	-0.113*

Note: * $p < .05$, ** $p < .10$.

Source: The Schools Database.

Figure 8.3: Predicted Subject Take-up by Transition Year Participation (Odds ratios compared with non-participants)

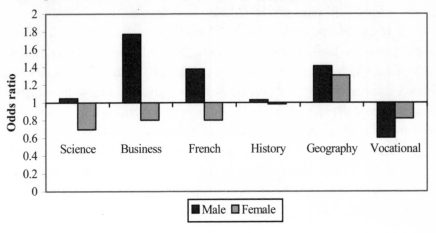

Leaving Cert subjects

Note: Derived from models in Table 8.2.

The pattern for business subjects and French take-up differs by gender. Male students who have taken Transition Year are more likely than non-participants to take a business subject and (to a lesser extent) French for the Leaving Cert. The pattern for business subjects may relate to greater exposure to work-related learning and enterprise-related activities (such as mini-companies) in the course of Transition Year rather than to the prevalence of business as an academic subject within the programme since under half of schools provide business subjects as part of Transition Year (see Chapter Four). It would appear, therefore, that taking part in Transition Year has an important influence on young people's subsequent route through the senior cycle. Its impact on course choice within higher education is discussed in section 8.4 below.

8.3 LEAVING CERTIFICATE PERFORMANCE

8.3.1 Overall Leaving Certificate performance

Leaving Certificate performance was measured using a grade point average (GPA), which involved scoring each examination grade from 0 to 28 and averaging the total scores over the number of exam subjects taken (see Ap-

pendix 8.1 for details). Figure 8.4 indicates the "raw" grade point average
of Transition Year participants and non-participants by gender. It is clear
that among both boys and girls, those who take the programme tend to
achieve higher raw grades (by over 2 grade points per subject) than non-
participants in their exams. Furthermore, those who have taken Transition
Year achieve higher grades than their counterparts from similar social class
backgrounds, although the performance gap is greater for those from higher
professional than from semi/unskilled manual backgrounds (1.7 compared
with 0.9 grade points). Performance differences between Transition Year
participants and non-participants are also found within school sectors, with
Transition Year students achieving higher grades than their counterparts
within secondary, vocational and community/comprehensive schools. The
one exception to higher performance among Transition Year students is
found in predominantly working-class schools where participants achieve
0.5 grade points lower than non-participants compared with a performance
gap of over 2 grade points in favour of participants in other schools. [12]

Figure 8.4: Leaving Certificate performance (Grade Point Average) by
Transition Year take-up and gender

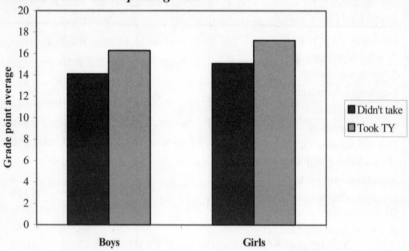

Source: The Schools Database.

---

[12] It should be noted that the difference between Transition Year participants and non-
participants in working-class schools is not statistically significant and that the number of
students taking Transition Year in these schools is relatively small.

Table 8.3: Leaving Certificate examination performance and
Transition Year participation (Multilevel regression model based on
4,434 students within 108 schools)

	Model 1	Model 2	Model 3
Constant	13.860	14.770	14.660
Gender	1.096*	0.233*	0.215
(Ref.: Male)			
Transition Year	1.284*	0.639*	0.605*
TY*female	0.710	0.245	0.253
(Ref.: Did not take TY)			
Family background:			
Higher professional		0.471*	0.411*
Lower professional		0.371*	0.324*
Other non-manual		0.054	0.025
Skilled manual		0.087	0.056
(Ref.: Semi/unskilled manual)			
Parents Third level		0.183**	0.154
(Ref: Other education)			
Age		−0.362*	−0.387*
Academic background:			
Ability test score		0.030*	0.030*
Junior Cert performance		2.558*	2.468*
Student attitudes:			
Academic self-image			0.410*
Positive interaction			−0.112
Negative interaction			−0.321*
School satisfaction			−0.040
School recreation			0.052
Low attendance			−0.250*
(Ref.: Average/good attendance)			
Vocational subjects			0.040
Unclear occupational aspirations			0.110
(Ref.: Specified occupation)			
Aspire to Leaving Cert			0.185
Aspire to Certificate			0.073
Aspire to Degree			0.454*
(Ref.: Aspire to Junior Cert)			
School-level variance	5.088*	0.566*	0.565*
Student-level variance	25.820*	6.168*	6.067*

Note: * p<.05, **p<.10. *Source*: The Schools Database.

Chapter Three has shown that students who take Transition Year differ from those who do not in a number of respects which are likely to affect exam performance. The performance gap described so far may, therefore, be due to the kind of students taking the programme rather than the effect of Transition Year per se. Multilevel models were used to examine the relationship between Transition Year take-up and exam grades controlling for these initial differences between the two groups. These techniques allow us to explore: firstly, whether Transition Year participants outperform other students because they are of initially higher ability/performance; secondly, whether programme participants outperform other students because they are "positively selected", that is, they have more positive views of, and orientation towards, school; and thirdly, whether the performance difference is attributable to the types of schools that provide the programme.

The models presented in Table 8.3 allow us to examine the relationship between Transition Year participation and Leaving Cert performance, controlling for objective and subjective student characteristics. The first model shows the difference between the two groups before differences in background are considered. Students who had taken part in Transition Year outscored their counterparts by over a grade point per subject (controlling for gender) (Table 8.3, Model 1). This is broadly consistent with the difference found in the NCCA study (Millar and Kelly, 1999). There is no evidence that the "effect" of Transition Year differs for males and females. The variance terms indicate that, controlling for Transition Year participation and gender, both schools and students vary in their average Leaving Cert grades.

Model 2 in Table 8.3 explores the effects of Transition Year controlling for family socio-economic background, age and prior ability/performance. As might be expected, Leaving Cert performance is strongly structured by social class and parental education, with those from professional backgrounds and/or those whose parents have third-level education achieving the highest exam results. Older students are found to under-perform in the Leaving Cert relative to younger members of the cohort. It should be noted that the age effect is apparent when Transition Year participation is controlled for; that is, students tend to achieve lower grades if they are older than the student cohort within which they are located (whether Transition Year participants or non-participants). This may be due to the fact that these students have been "kept back" earlier in their schooling career because of educational underperformance. As might be expected, students who achieve higher Junior Cert grades also achieve higher Leaving Cert grades. More surprisingly, perhaps, ability test score in third year is positively associated with Leaving Cert performance, even controlling for Junior Cert grades, although the effect is quite small. When parental background, age and prior ability/performance are taken into account, Transition Year participants are found to outperform non-participants by 0.6 grade points per subject. While this is about half of the initial effect size, the effect is significant and substantive.

The data used for this study contained a range of measures on the attitudes and aspirations of the students prior to their Junior Certificate and prior to the point at which they made the decision about Transition Year participation (see Chapter One). A number of attitudinal factors are associated with Leaving Cert performance, even controlling for Junior Cert performance. Grades are higher among those who aspire to a third-level degree and among those who have a more positive view of their own abilities (Table 8.3, Model 3). Students who have experienced negative interaction with teachers under-perform in their exam as do those who have poor attendance records at junior cycle. Controlling for student attitudes in third year reduces the coefficient for Transition Year only very slightly; participants continue to outperform non-participants by 0.6 grade points per exam subject.

Chapter Two has illustrated important differences in the types of schools that provide Transition Year and whether they provide the programme on a compulsory or optional basis. It may be the case that the performance difference between participants and non-participants is, in fact, attributable to the types of schools that provide the programme and the basis on which the programme is provided. Table 8.4 distinguishes between compulsory and optional Transition Year programmes in exploring their effects on performance. Raw grade point averages are higher for those who take a compulsory Transition Year programme rather than an optional one (Table 8.4, Model 1); however, this is due to the higher socio-economic profile of students in these schools since the difference is no longer significant when parental background and prior performance is taken into account (see Model 2). Controlling for family background, prior attitudes and performance, the effects of participating in a compulsory programme resemble the effects of participation in an optional programme with a performance gain for students in both kinds of programme (Table 8.4, Model 3).

A possible explanation of the performance gap is that schools who decide to provide Transition Year differ from other schools in terms of the kinds of characteristics which might promote performance; in other words, schools that provide Transition Year are more academically effective and higher grades among Transition Year students merely reflect effectiveness on the part of the school. A range of factors which are known to be associated with academic effectiveness in the Irish context (see Smyth, 1999) were controlled for (analyses not shown here). These included: academic climate, ability grouping, nature of teacher–student interaction, student involvement in the school, timing of subject choice, disciplinary climate, subject specialisation and nature of guidance counsellor involvement. The Transition Year effect remains remarkably stable at around 0.6 grade points per subject, indicating that the performance difference does not appear to be due to the fact that the programme is provided in more academically effective schools.

Possible unmeasured school differences relating to the type of Transition Year provision can also be controlled for by analysing only the 48 schools in the sample within which Transition Year participation is optional. The estimates of the difference in performance between Transition Year participants and non-participants are similar to those found in the earlier analyses, indicating that Transition Year participation differentiates among those attending the same school (see Table 8.5).

Table 8.4: Leaving Cert performance — a comparison of compulsory and optional Transition Year programmes (Multilevel regression model based on 4,434 students within 108 schools)

	Model 1	Model 2	Model 3
Constant	13.820	14.770	14.660
Gender	1.100*	0.239*	0.222**
(Ref.: Male)			
TY compulsory	1.550*	0.705*	0.663*
TY comp.*female	0.632	0.149	0.150
TY optional	1.200*	0.583*	0.550*
TY optional*female	0.789	0.326	0.338
(Ref.: Did not take TY)			
Family background:			
Higher professional		0.470*	0.410*
Lower professional		0.372*	0.324*
Other non-manual		0.054	0.025
Skilled manual		0.087	0.056
(Ref.: Semi/unskilled manual)			
Parents Third level		0.182**	0.154
(Ref.: Other education)			
Age		−0.363*	−0.388*
Academic background:			
Ability test score		0.029*	0.029*
Junior Cert performance		2.558*	2.468*
Student attitudes:			
Academic self-image			0.409*
Positive interaction			−0.112
Negative interaction			−0.321*
School satisfaction			−0.041
School recreation			0.052
Low attendance			−0.250*
(Ref.: Average/good attendance)			
Vocational subjects			0.040
Unclear occupational aspirations			0.103
(Ref.: Specified occupation)			
Aspire to Leaving Cert			0.186
Aspire to Certificate			0.073
Aspire to Degree			0.455*
(Ref.: Aspire to Junior Cert)			
School-level variance	4.357*	0.573*	0.571*
Student-level variance	25.290*	6.166*	6.065*

Note: * p<.05, ** p<.10. *Source*: The Schools Database.

Table 8.5: Leaving Certificate Performance: schools with optional Transition Year (Multilevel regression model based on 2,312 students within 48 schools)

	Model 1	Model 2	Model 3
Constant	13.980	14.650	14.090
Gender	1.417*	0.341*	0.386*
(Ref.: Male)			
Transition Year	1.282*	0.668*	0.601*
TY*female	0.554	0.189	0.263
(Ref.: Did not take TY)			
Family background:			
Higher professional		0.600*	0.475*
Lower professional		0.398*	0.325*
Other non-manual		0.202	0.134
Skilled manual		0.300	0.245
(Ref.: Semi/unskilled manual)			
Parents Third level		0.122	0.108
(Ref.: Other education)			
Age		−0.331*	−0.384*
Academic background:			
Ability test score		0.029*	0.029*
Junior Cert performance		2.605*	2.554*
Student attitudes:			
Academic self-image			0.297**
Positive interaction			−0.052
Negative interaction			−0.290*
School satisfaction			−0.138*
School recreation			0.051
Low attendance			−0.373*
(Ref.: Average/good attendance)			
Vocational subjects			0.100
Unclear occupational aspirations			0.031
(Ref.: Specify occupation)			
Aspire to Leaving Cert			0.085
Aspire to Certificate			−0.127
Aspire to Degree			0.155
(Ref.: Aspire to Junior Cert)			
School-level variance	3.516*	0.423*	0.369*
Student-level variance	26.110*	6.022*	5.929*

Note: * p<.05, ** p<.10. *Source*: The Schools Database.

The nature of the performance gap between Transition Year participants and non-participants is summarised in Figure 8.5. The figure shows the grade differences between the two groups controlling progressively for student background and performance, student attitudes and school characteristics. The first set of columns relates to the total sample (including all students whether they are in a school providing Transition Year or not) while the second set of columns relates only to those schools in which the programme is optional. Around half of the "raw" performance gap between the two groups is attributable to the kinds of students taking the programme but substantial differences remain when these initial differences are controlled for.

Figure 8.5: Predicted performance difference (Grade point average) between Transition Year participants and non-participants

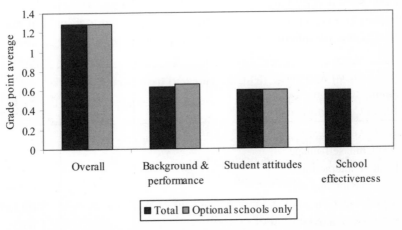

Note: Derived from models in Tables 8.3 and 8.4.

The methodology appropriate for estimating the effect of a particular programme or intervention on participants has been the subject of much debate (see D'Agostino, 1998; Conniffe et al., 2000). In particular, it has been argued that the kinds of techniques used so far in this chapter may not provide an accurate estimate of the effect if the participants and non-participants differ markedly in terms of key characteristics. Propensity score matching techniques have been developed in order to provide a way of more closely comparing "like with like" in examining the impact of participation in a particular programme. Such techniques were used in analysing Leaving Cert performance both among all students in the sample and among students in schools with an optional Transition Year programme (see Appendix 8.2 for further details). The analysis indicated that the performance gap between participants and non-participants is apparent even when participants and non-participants are matched in terms of their characteristics at the end of junior cycle.

8.3.2 Leaving Certificate performance in specific subjects

The previous analyses related to Leaving Cert performance as a composite measure. Table 8.6 indicates the raw performance gap across the different Leaving Cert subjects; positive values indicate that Transition Year participants achieve higher grades than non-participants in their Leaving Cert exam. Only those subjects taken by more than ten per cent of the cohort are included in order to provide more reliable estimates. Transition Year participants significantly outperform non-participants in all subjects except Engineering, Construction Studies and Accountancy. Performance gaps appear to be somewhat larger in Art and French and less apparent in the practical subjects and Irish. The pattern for Engineering, Construction Studies and Accountancy may relate to the fact that these subjects are provided in only a very small minority of Transition Year programmes (see Chapter Four). However, the performance differences in individual subjects should be interpreted with caution since they reflect not only differences in the characteristics of Transition Year participants and non-participants but, in the case of many subjects, the factors influencing take-up of that subject.

Analyses were conducted on the factors influencing performance in English and Maths, subjects selected because they are taken by the vast majority of students. Raw exam results indicate that Transition Year participants outperform non-participants by over 1.5 grade points in both English and Maths (see Figure 8.6). Fifty-four per cent of the difference in English, and 60 per cent of the difference in Maths, is accounted for by differences between participants and non-participants in family background, prior performance and student attitudes. All else being equal, participants outperform Transition Year non-participants by 0.6–0.7 grade points in English and Maths.

Table 8.6: *Raw performance difference (Grade points) between Transition Year participants and non-participants by Leaving Cert subject*

Subject	Performance Gap (TY participant – non-participant)
Irish	1.58***
English	2.11***
Maths	2.26***
History	2.11***
Geography	1.99***
French	3.02***
German	2.06***
Art	3.25***
Physics	1.63**
Chemistry	2.72***
Biology	2.92***
Engineering	0.14
Technical Graphics	1.32*
Construction Studies	0.70
Accountancy	0.83
Business Organisation	2.06***

Note: *** $p < .001$; ** $p < .01$; * $p < .05$. *Source*: The Schools Database.

Figure 8.6: *Predicted performance gap (Grade points) in English and Maths*

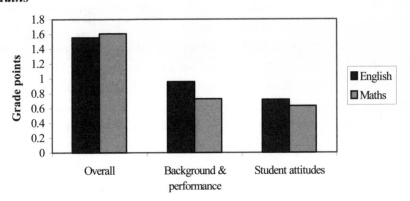

Source: The Schools Database.

8.3.3 Who benefits from Transition Year?

The analysis so far has focused on examining the *average* effect of Transition Year on Leaving Certificate performance. The lack of difference in the Transition Year effect between male and female students has also been highlighted. However, it is worth exploring whether Transition Year yields more benefits for some groups of students than others and in some school contexts rather than others.

Across all students in the sample, no difference by family background (either parental social class or education) is found in the effect of Transition Year on exam performance. Similarly, the effect does not differ by the Junior Cert performance of the student. However, a significant interaction was found between the social class composition of the school and the effect of Transition Year; the performance gap between Transition Year participants and non-participants was found to be less in predominantly working-class schools than in other schools (see Figure 8.7).

Figure 8.7: Predicted Leaving Cert performance difference (Grade Point Average) by social class composition of school (compared with schools with no Transition Year programme)

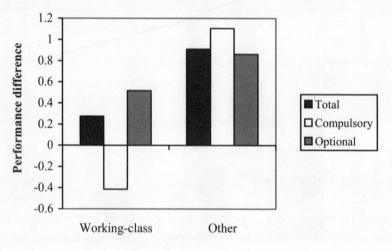

School composition

Note: This controls for gender, individual social class, parental education, age and Junior Cert performance.

Source: The Schools Database.

On closer investigation, the pattern appears to differ between schools where Transition Year is compulsory and those where it is optional. The performance gap in favour of Transition Year participants is not apparent in schools serving a predominantly working-class student intake where the programme is compulsory. In schools where Transition Year is optional, the "benefits" of participation are somewhat reduced but the difference in the Transition Year performance gap between predominantly working-class and other schools is not statistically significant.

Analyses were also carried on optional schools only to determine whether the Transition Year effect varied across different types of students. There was a significant interaction between Junior Cert performance and the Transition Year effect with Transition Year having a stronger effect for initially lower-achieving students (see Figure 8.8).

Figure 8.8: Predicted performance gap by Junior Cert performance (schools with optional Transition Year only)

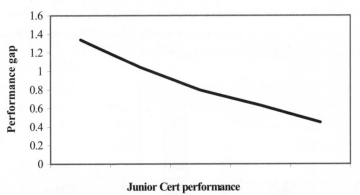

Junior Cert performance

Note: This controls for gender, family background, prior ability and social mix of the school.
Source: The Schools Database.

In sum, Transition Year participants tend to achieve higher Leaving Cert exam grades on average, even when initial differences between participants and non-participants are taken into account. However, there is tentative evidence that the benefits of Transition Year may differ across students and schools. Students in predominantly working-class schools where Transition Year is compulsory do not seem to secure the same performance gains as those in other school types. On the other hand, lower achieving students who opt voluntarily for the programme appear to achieve somewhat higher performance gains.

8.4 ENTRY TO HIGHER EDUCATION

Three-quarters of the Leaving Certificate students in the sample applied for a higher education place through the Central Applications Office (CAO) system, whether at certificate/diploma or degree level. Girls were more likely than boys to apply for higher education (see Table 8.7, Model 1). Students who had taken Transition Year were more than twice as likely as other students to have applied for higher education.

Third-level applications are strongly structured by parental background with students from higher professional backgrounds being three times as likely as those from semi/unskilled manual backgrounds to apply, even controlling for Junior Cert performance. As might be expected, Junior Cert performance is predictive of third-level applications, with higher achieving students being more likely to apply for college. Controlling for parental background and prior performance, Transition Year participants are almost twice as likely to apply for higher education as non-participants (Model 2, Table 8.7).

Student attitudes prior to the Junior Cert are also predictive of later decisions regarding educational participation. Students with poor attendance records at junior cycle are less likely to apply for higher education as are those who specialised in vocational subjects for the Junior Cert (Model 3, Table 8.7). Educational aspirations in third year are significantly associated with third-level applications, with those who aspire to a degree being six times more likely to apply for higher education than those who plan to leave school before the Leaving Cert. Even controlling for student attitudes, Transition Year participants are more likely than non-participants to apply for higher education, although the difference is reduced somewhat in magnitude (to a ratio of 1.6) (see Figure 8.9).

Table 8.7: Third-level applications and Transition Year participation (Multilevel logistic regression based on 4,434 students in 108 schools)

	Model 1	Model 2	Model 3
Constant	0.775	1.179	0.953*
Gender	0.235*	0.044	−0.477*
(Ref.: Male)			
Transition Year	0.728*	0.688*	0.472*
TY*female	0.091	−0.069	0.138
(Ref.: Did not take TY)			
Family background:			
Higher professional		1.099*	0.970*
Lower professional		0.990*	0.905*
Other non-manual		0.593*	0.540*
Skilled manual		0.320*	0.294*
(Ref.: Semi/unskilled manual)			
Parents Third level		0.091	0.004
(Ref.: Other education)			
Age		−0.108	−0.097
Academic background:			
Ability test score		0.026*	0.027*
Junior Cert performance		0.944*	0.813*
Student attitudes:			
Academic self-image			0.211
Positive interaction			0.163
Negative interaction			−0.035
School satisfaction			−0.041
School recreation			−0.012
Low attendance			−0.440*
(Ref.: Average/good attendance)			
Vocational subjects			−0.592*
Unclear occupational aspirations			0.226
(Ref.: Specify occupation)			
Aspire to Leaving Cert			0.562*
Aspire to Certificate			1.206*
Aspire to Degree			1.606*
(Ref.: Aspire to Junior Cert)			
School-level variance	0.913*	0.687*	0.681*

Note: * p<.05. *Source*: The Schools Database.

Figure 8.9: Predicted applications to higher education — the impact of Transition Year participation (Odds ratios compared to not participating in Transition Year)

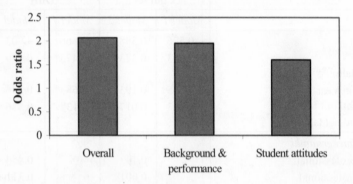

Note: Derived from models in Table 8.7.

Actual entry patterns to third-level education reflect not only application patterns but also Leaving Cert performance and take-up of certain subjects designated as requirements for course entry. Analyses in Table 8.8 contrast the chances of being offered and accepting a place with all other possible outcomes (including not applying, not being offered a place and refusing a place). Figure 8.10 shows the impact of Transition Year on entry to higher education. The first set of columns control for student background and attitudes while the second set incorporate an additional control for Leaving Cert performance. The figure indicates that Transition Year participants are 1.3 times more likely to enter higher education and almost twice as likely to enter degree courses as non-participants. However, this is found to be due to the Leaving Certificate grade advantage secured by participants as the impact of Transition Year participation becomes non-significant when Leaving Cert grades are taken into account.[13] In overall terms, the performance gain from Transition Year participation appears to facilitate higher entry levels to third-level education.

---

[13] For degree courses, the effect of Transition Year is significantly different for males and females. The interaction term becomes significant when Junior Cert performance is entered into the model so it appears that Transition Year females are less likely to enter higher education than might be expected given their previous performance.

Table 8.8: Higher education entry and Transition Year participation (Multilevel logistic regression based on 4,434 students in 108 schools)

	All Third–level Courses		Degree Courses Only	
	Model 1	*Model 2*	*Model 1*	*Model 2*
Constant	−0.526	−0.398	−1.866*	−4.903
Gender (Ref.: Male)	0.053	−0.273*	0.473*	0.179
Transition Year	0.265*	−0.193	0.683*	0.346
TY*female (Ref.: Did not take TY)	0.163	0.017	−0.132	−0.536*
Family background:				
Higher professional		−0.143		0.454
Lower professional		−0.001		0.311
Other non-manual		−0.128		0.143
Skilled manual (Ref.: Semi/unskilled manual)		−0.199		−0.438
Parents Third level (Ref.: Other education)		−0.268*		−0.226
Age		0.137		0.259**
Academic background:				
Ability test score		0.002		0.001
Junior Cert performance		0.062		−0.056
Student attitudes:				
Academic self-image		0.008		−0.007
Positive interaction		−0.045		−0.003
Negative interaction		0.022		−0.027
School satisfaction		−0.074		−0.132
School recreation		−0.021		0.085
Low attendance (Ref.: Average/good attendance)		−0.171		−0.344
Vocational subjects		0.170		0.180
Unclear occupational aspirations (Ref.: Specify occupation)		0.205**		0.240
Aspire to Leaving Cert		0.227		0.418
Aspire to Certificate		0.648*		0.623
Aspire to Degree (Ref.: Aspire to Junior Cert)		0.233		0.894**
Leaving Cert performance		0.369*		0.863*
School variance	0.325*	0.141*	0.507*	0.115**

Note: * p<.05, ** p<.10. *Source*: The Schools Database.

Figure 8.10: Predicted entry levels to higher education — the impact of Transition Year participation (Odds ratios compared to non-participation)

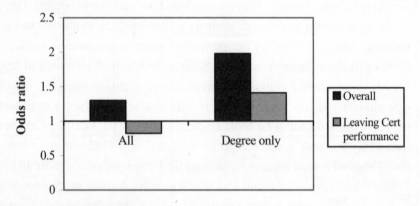

Note: Derived from the models in Table 8.8.

8.4.1 Course choice within third-level education

Section 8.2 has indicated the way in which participation in Transition Year can influence the selection of certain Leaving Certificate subjects, especially among male students. It is also possible to assess whether Transition Year participants differ from non-participants in the types of courses they take within higher education. Table 8.9 presents a set of models analysing the factors influencing course entry at third-level; each course area is contrasted with all of the other course areas.[14] In keeping with previous research (see, for example, Clancy, 2001), there are significant gender differences in course choice within third-level education. Young women are over-represented in Arts/Social Science courses and under-represented in Engineering courses, even controlling for their prior subject take-up and attitudes to subject areas. Family background no longer has a significant effect on course choice when educational performance and subject take-up are taken into account. Similarly, Junior Cert performance does not have a direct effect once subsequent take-up and performance are controlled for.

---

[14] A multinomial logit model was not suitable as the coefficients for Transition Year participation were sensitive to the choice of a base category.

Attitudes to subjects prior to the Junior Cert exam are found to be predictive of course entry. Those with a preference for Maths/Science subjects are more likely to enter Engineering and Science courses and less likely to enter "other" courses (such as Law and Architecture). Having a preference for vocational subjects is also predictive of entry to Engineering. Students with an orientation to English and similar subjects are more likely to enter Arts/Social Science and "other" courses and less likely to enter science courses. In keeping with previous research, senior cycle subject take-up is predictive of later course entry (see Smyth and Hannan, 2002). Those who took a science subject for Leaving Cert are more likely to enter science at third-level and less likely to enter business. Those who took a business subject for Leaving Cert are more likely to enter a business course and less likely to enter science or engineering courses. Students who took a vocational course are more likely to enter Engineering while those who have taken History are more likely to enter Arts/Social Science courses. Geography take-up is not significantly associated with any particular field of education at third-level. Leaving Cert performance is somewhat higher among those entering Arts/Social Science and other courses and lower among those entering Engineering courses. This is likely to reflect the relative balance between degree and diploma courses within the particular fields as well as the points requirements for individual courses.

The differences between Transition Year participants and non-participants in their course choices are presented in Figure 8.11. Controlling for prior performance, subject take-up and attitudes to subject areas, taking Transition Year reduces the chances of taking Engineering courses for male students. For females, it appears that taking Transition Year somewhat reduces gender segregation in entry to engineering. Taking Transition Year appears to increase the chances of entering Business and Arts courses for male students but not for female students. These patterns may relate to the kinds of skills fostered by the Transition Year programme, for example, through participation in mini-company modules. There are no significant differences between participants and non-participants in entry to science or "other" courses.

Table 8.9: Third-level course choice and Transition Year participation (4,434 students within 108 schools)

	Science (incl. Medicine, Computing)	Engineering	Business	Other	Arts/Social Science
Constant	-1.999	-0.728	-2.392	-2.608	-2.108
Gender	-0.059	-2.831*	0.409*	0.953*	1.619*
Transition Year	0.133	-1.061*	0.768*	0.435	0.894*
TY*female	-0.155	1.654*	-0.983*	-0.579	-0.787*
Family background:					
Higher professional	-0.179	-0.006	0.056	0.056	0.066
Lower professional	-0.319	0.126	-0.051	0.054	0.305
Other non–manual	-0.165	-0.231	0.363	-0.334	0.164
Skilled manual	-0.122	0.321	-0.022	-0.485	0.205
Parents Third level	-0.087	0.126	-0.104	0.090	0.106
Ability test score	0.010	0.006	-0.019*	0.005	0.001
Junior Cert subject take–up:					
Science	0.414	-0.314	0.443	-0.494	-0.535
Business Studies	0.209	-0.298	0.082	0.365	-0.282
Vocational subject(s)	-0.296	-0.122	-0.483	0.389	-0.014
History	-0.209	-0.079	1.062*	-0.906*	-0.168
Geography	-0.054	0.309	-0.687	0.645	0.412

Attitudes in third year:					
Maths/Science pref.	0.320*	0.238*	-0.102	-0.215*	-0.339*
English preference	-0.278*	-0.100	-0.089	0.301*	0.249*
Vocational preference	-0.024	0.239*	0.012	0.168	-0.282*
Junior Cert performance	0.169	-0.329*	0.040	0.041	-0.105
Leaving Cert subject take–up:					
Science subject(s)	0.988*	0.357	-0.629*	-0.160	0.111
Business subject(s)	-0.848*	-0.619*	1.802*	-0.193	-0.439*
Vocational subject(s)	-0.975*	1.374*	-1.114*	0.449	-1.115*
History	-0.550*	-0.448*	-0.045	0.103	0.723*
Geography	-0.049	-0.275	-0.003	0.071	0.173
Leaving Cert performance	-0.065*	-0.124*	-0.058**	0.125*	0.174*

Note: * p<.05, ** p<.10.

Source: The Schools Database.

Figure 8.11: Course choice at higher education (Odds ratio of entering particular courses among Transition Year participants compared with non-participants)

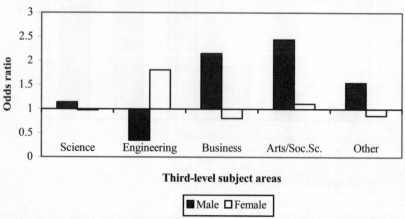

Third-level subject areas

Note: Derived from models in Table 8.9.

In sum, students who have taken Transition Year are more likely to apply for, and enter, higher education, particularly at the degree level. When they do enter higher education, they tend to take different kinds of courses than non-participants. In particular, Transition Year appears to channel young men away from Engineering courses towards Arts, Social Science and Business courses.

8.5 LABOUR MARKET INTEGRATION

Taking Transition Year may impact not only on young people's educational career but on their relationship with the labour market. Some of the debate about Transition Year has centred on the tendency of Transition Year students to engage in part-time employment (see, for example, Skills Initiative Unit, 2002). Data from the Annual School Leavers' Survey allow us to explore whether Transition Year students are, in fact, more likely to engage in paid employment than students in other year groups. Respondents were asked whether they had worked in each of the school years from first to Leaving Cert year. Figure 8.12 shows the proportion who engaged in part-time work during term-time by school year. Part-time employment increases dramatically between junior and senior cycle and is particularly high in Transition Year.

Figure 8.12: Part-time employment by school year

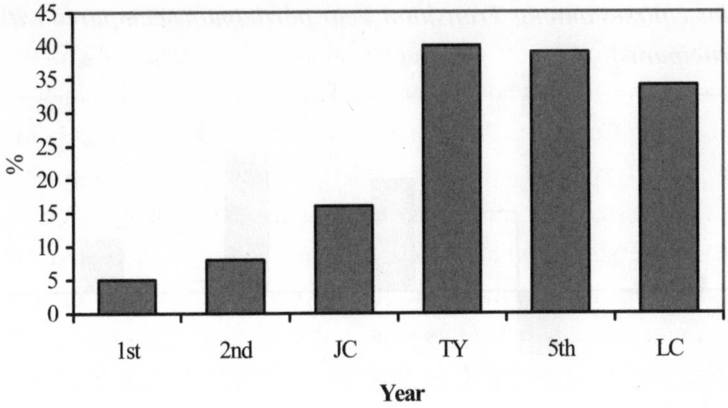

Source: Annual School Leavers' Survey, 1999.

Working during Transition Year is also associated with working in fifth year; 83 per cent of those who worked during Transition Year also worked in fifth year compared with 23 per cent of those who had taken Transition Year but not worked. Furthermore, almost two-thirds (64 per cent) of those who worked in Transition Year also worked in their Leaving Cert year. When Transition Year participants and non-participants are compared, those who had taken Transition Year are much more likely to work in fifth year than non-participants (48 per cent compared with 35 per cent). However, this is related to whether students worked in Transition Year. Students who took Transition Year but did not work during the year are less likely than Transition Year non-participants to work during fifth year.

The significant involvement of Transition Year students in part-time work and its implications for their continuing employment may be of concern given the association between part-time work and educational underperformance in the Leaving Cert exam (McCoy, Smyth, forthcoming). Data from the Annual School Leavers' Survey allow us to explore whether the tendency of Transition Year students to work part-time cancels out the performance benefits from the programme discussed earlier in this chapter. Because detailed information on exam grades was not available from the School Leavers' Survey, analyses distinguish between those who received four or more higher level grades at Leaving Cert and those who achieved fewer than four higher level grades. Information on Junior Cert performance was not available so the analysis relates to differences in Leaving Cert grades rather than differences in relative progress over the senior cycle. Figure 8.13 depicts the relative chances of achieving four or more higher level grades, controlling for parental social class. The specified groups are contrasted against those who did not take Transition Year and did not work in their Leaving Cert year. Students who took Transition Year and did not work in their Leaving Cert year have the highest performance levels. Among female students, those who took Transition Year but worked in sixth year have similar grade levels to Transition Year non-participants who did not work. Among male students, the performance gain from taking the programme appears to be more than cancelled out by the negative effect of working in their Leaving Cert year with Transition Year participants who worked doing significantly worse than non-participants who did not work. The differential patterns by gender are likely to relate to the longer average hours worked by male students and the greater tendency of female students to engage in more irregular and flexible forms of employment such as babysitting (see McCoy, Smyth, forthcoming).

Figure 8.13: Predicted chances of obtaining four or more higher Leaving Cert grades by Transition Year participation and employment in Leaving Cert year (compared with Transition Year non-participants not in employment)

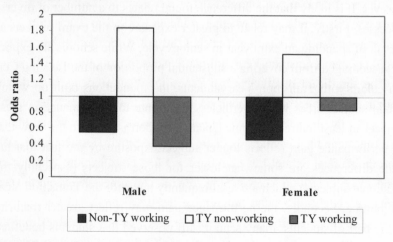

Source: Derived from the Annual School Leavers' Survey, 1999.

Data from the School Leavers' Survey also allow us to look at employment patterns after leaving school. Earlier analyses indicated that Transition Year participants are more likely to apply for, and enter, higher education. These findings were confirmed by analysis of the School Leavers' Survey (results not shown here). In terms of young people who entered the labour market directly on leaving school, unemployment rates are only slightly lower among Transition Year participants than non-participants one year after leaving school (6 per cent compared with 9 per cent) and the unemployment differences between the two groups are not significant when gender, family background and performance are taken into account. Transition Year participants are somewhat more likely to enter non-manual than manual jobs after leaving school. However, these differences are not significant when social background and gender are taken into account.

8.6 Conclusions

This chapter has explored the differences between students who have taken Transition Year and those who have not taken the programme in relation to a range of outcomes. It is clear that Transition Year participants achieve higher average Leaving Cert exam grades and are more likely to go on to third-level education than non-participants, even controlling for initial differences between the two groups of students.

It is more difficult to infer the reasons behind this performance gain, however. It is likely that the difference found relates to a number of diverse processes. Firstly, it may relate to greater exposure to the exam subjects as a result of spending an extra year in senior cycle. While schools are explicitly discouraged from covering a substantial proportion of the Leaving Cert curriculum with Transition Year students, the foundations built up within certain subject areas will nevertheless contribute to performance in these subjects, at least indirectly. Some tentative support is given to the view that the performance gain reflects longer subject exposure by the fact that the grade differences are somewhat lower for those subjects (especially the vocational subjects) which are less frequently a part of the Transition Year programme. Secondly, the performance gain may reflect greater maturity on the part of students; many school staff observed that students benefited from the extra year in developmental terms (see Chapter Six). While the programme may contribute to maturity in terms of personal and social development, age per se does not enhance Leaving Cert performance since older students within particular cohorts tend to under-perform relative to

their peers. Thirdly, Transition Year participation may help students to select Leaving Cert subjects which better reflect their interests and abilities
and thus contribute to higher performance. Fourthly, students may develop
a more self-directed approach to learning and study harder (or more effectively) for the Leaving Certificate exam.

While Transition Year participation results in an average performance gain, there is some variation in the effects of the programme across
schools and students. Participation in Transition Year is associated with
an increase in student involvement in paid employment outside school
and this involvement continues over the senior cycle for many students.
Thus, involvement in paid work is found to cancel out the positive benefits of Transition Year in terms of performance for male students. In addition, the performance gain is less for students in predominantly working-class schools with compulsory Transition Year. Furthermore, student
drop-out tends to be higher in schools with a compulsory Transition
Year. It may be the case that an obligatory extra year in schools causes
some students to become disaffected and leave school early or under-
perform academically if they do remain within the system.

In addition to influencing educational performance, Transition Year
participation appears to impact on the kinds of subjects students take at
Leaving Cert level and on entry to higher education. Male students, in
particular, tend to be channelled towards the business and humanities
areas to a greater extent. This pattern relates only in part to the relative
emphasis within Transition Year programmes on the different subjects
areas (see Chapter Four) and may be due to the kinds of skills fostered
by the programme.

It should be acknowledged that, while our findings indicate clear differences in academic outcomes between participants and non-participants,
the Transition Year programme is not explicitly intended to promote Leaving Cert performance and so cannot be assessed by these criteria alone. Unfortunately, the data are not available to assess the impact of participation
on the personal development and "soft skills" of students. Stakeholder perceptions of the success of the programme in these respects are broadly positive (Chapters Six and Seven). However, more information is needed on the
extent to which Transition Year impacts on social skills development, all
else being equal, and whether such effects are evident in the long term.

APPENDIX 8.1: DEFINITION OF VARIABLES

Variables	Description
Outcomes	
School drop-out	Dichotomous variable where 1=left school before the Leaving Cert exam but after the Junior Cert exam.
Leaving Cert performance	Points were allocated to each exam grades; the points ranged from 0 for E, F or NG grades to 20 for a higher level A1 grade. These points were averaged over all exam subjects taken.
Leaving Cert subject take-up	Science subjects — 1 or more of: Biology, Physics, Chemistry, Physics-Chemistry.
	Business subjects — 1 or more of: Accountancy, Business Organisation, Economics, Agricultural Economics.
	French — took LC French.
	History — took LC History.
	Geography — took LC Geography.
	Vocational subject — 1 or more of: Engineering, Technical Drawing, Construction Studies.
Higher education application	Dummy variable where 1=applied for a Certificate, Diploma or Degree course through the CAO.
Higher education entry	Dummy variable where 1=offered and accepted a place on a Certificate, Diploma or Degree course through the CAO.
Third-level course choice	Course accepted grouped into: Science (including Medicine and Computing), Engineering, Business, Arts/Social Science and other (Art, Architecture, Agriculture, Law, Education and vocational courses). For more detailed information on the categories used, see Smyth and Hannan (2002).
Transition Year	
Took Transition Year	Dummy variable where 1=spent three years at senior cycle without repeating the Leaving Cert within a school which provided Transition Year.
Compulsory TY provision	Dummy variable where 1=all students in the school took Transition Year.
Optional TY provision	Dummy variable where 1=some students in the school took Transition Year.

Variables	Description
Student Background	
Gender	Dummy variable where 1= female.
Social class: Higher professional Lower professional Non-manual Skilled manual	Census Social Class categories based on the occupational status of parents; contrasted against semi/unskilled manual workers.
Parental education: Parents Third Level	Dummy variables where 1=at least one parent had a third-level education (either at Certificate, Diploma or Degree level).
Age	Age at end of junior cycle.
Ability test score	VRNA, combined verbal reasoning and numerical ability scores; centred on its mean value.
Junior Cert performance	Points were allocated to each exam grades; the points ranged from 0 for E, F or NG grades to 10 for a higher level A grade. These points were averaged over all exam subjects taken.
Took relevant subject for Junior Cert	Set of dummy variables: LC science — Science; LC business — Business Studies; LC French — French; LC History — History; LC Geography — Geography; LC vocational subject — Materials Technology, Metalwork or Technical Graphics.
Student Attitudes	
Academic Self-Image	Likert scale based on the following items: (1) I can do just about anything I set my mind to (2) I'm usually well ahead of others in my year in school (3) I am as good at school work as most other people my age (4) I'm hardly ever able to do what my teachers expect of me (reversed) (5) I'm usually well ahead of others in my class. Values range from 0 to 3.

Variables	Description
Positive teacher interaction	Likert scale based on frequency of following items: (1) Have you been told that your work is good? (2) Have you been asked questions in class? (3) Have you been praised for answering a difficult question correctly? (4) Have you been praised because your written work is well done? Ranges from 0 (low) to 3 (high).
Negative teacher interaction	Likert scale based on frequency of following items: (1) Have you been given out to because your work is untidy or not done on time? (2) Have you wanted to ask or answer questions in class but were ignored? (3) Have you been given out to for misbehaving in class? (4) Teachers pay more attention in class to what some students say than to others. (5) I find most teachers hard to talk to. Values range from 1 (low) to 4 (high).
School satisfaction	Extent to which agrees with the statement that: "For the most part, school life is a happy one for me"; values range from 1 (low) to 4 (high).
School recreation	Frequency of participation in school-organised sports and extracurricular activities (such as plays, debates etc.) in the previous two weeks. Values range from 0 (low) to 4 (high).
Absenteeism	Dummy variable where 1= pupil has poor/average attendance over previous year; contrasted against good attendance.
Vocational subjects	Dummy variable where 1=took two or more vocational subjects (Materials Technology, Metalwork, Technical Graphics and Home Economics) at Junior Cert.
Unclear occupational aspirations	Dummy variable where 1=no clear occupational preference at age 14.
Educational aspirations	Set of dummy variables where 1=aspire to Leaving Cert, Cert/Diploma and Degree qualifications respectively.

Variables	Description
Maths/Science orientation	Extent to which agrees with the statement that "I prefer subjects in which I have to work out problems such as Maths or Science". Scored from "strongly disagree" (1) to "strongly agree" (4).
English orientation	Extent to which agrees with the statement that "I have more confidence in dealing with a subject like English than with any Science subject". Scored from "strongly disagree" (1) to "strongly agree" (4).
Vocational orientation	Extent to which agrees with the statement that "I really like subjects where I can work with my hands, like woodwork or home economics". Scored from "strongly disagree" (1) to "strongly agree" (4).
Part-time work	
Part-time work (Schools Leavers' Survey)	Respondent engaged in any paid work during term-time while in specific years at school

APPENDIX 8.2: COMPARING TRANSITION YEAR PARTICIPANTS AND NON-PARTICIPANTS USING PROPENSITY SCORE MATCHING TECHNIQUES

Chapter Three has shown that students who take Transition Year differ from students who do not take the programme in relation to a number of characteristics, characteristics which are also likely to influence subsequent outcomes such as examination performance. Conventional regression methods correct for these initial differences by controlling for these factors in estimating the effect of participation in a particular programme on a specific outcome. However, it has been argued that such an approach may not accurately estimate the programme effect if participants and non-participants differ very markedly. Propensity score matching techniques involve matching participants and non-participants in terms of their characteristics prior to entry into the programme and are thus designed to compare "like with like" in examining the effect of a particular treatment on a specified outcome (see D'Agostino, 1998; Conniffe et al., 2000).

Two sets of analyses were conducted: the first relating to the impact of Transition Year participation on Leaving Cert performance among the whole sample, including those in schools where the programme is compulsory, optional or not provided; the second to the impact of Transition

Year participation on Leaving Cert performance among students in schools where the programme is optional. Transition Year participants were found to differ from non-participants in terms of their gender, family background, attitudes to school and Junior Cert performance (see Chapter Three), all variables known to be associated with Leaving Cert performance.

For the first set of analyses, a propensity score was derived by using gender, parental social class, parental education, age at Junior Cert, take-up of vocational subjects at junior cycle, educational aspirations and Junior Certificate performance to predict the probability of participation in Transition Year. In order to improve the balance among the covariates, interaction terms were fitted between parental class and education, vocational track and educational aspirations, and Junior Cert grades and vocational track. The sample was initially divided into ten strata (or "bins") of equal size on the basis of the propensity score. One stratum was found to be imbalanced in terms of the propensity score and was further subdivided yielding a total of eleven strata. All of the covariates balanced within all of the bins, with the exception of age in stratum seven and parental class in stratum ten. In addition, other factors (such as positive teacher-student interaction, school satisfaction and academic self-image) which were not included in the estimation of the propensity score were balanced within all of the strata.

Average Leaving Cert performance by Transition Year participation status was estimated within each stratum. In ten of the eleven strata, Transition Year participants had higher grades than non-participants. The average difference in performance between Transition Year participants and non-participants was just over 2 grade points per subject. The weighted average difference across strata was just over 1 grade point per subject, indicating that around half of the performance gap is due to the kinds of students taking the programme. In addition, Leaving Cert performance was regressed on Junior Cert performance and Transition Year participation within each stratum. The coefficient for programme participation (averaged across all strata) was 0.982 compared with an unadjusted coefficient of 1.164 if a regression model is estimated on the basis of the whole sample. In keeping with the multilevel regression analyses presented in the chapter, therefore, Transition Year participants have a definite performance advantage over non-participants.

In order to correct for possible unmeasured differences relating to the nature of Transition Year provision, the propensity score analysis was repeated for the subset of schools in which Transition Year is optional. Using the same covariates, the optimal balance was achieved by dividing the sample into eleven strata. The covariates were balanced across strata, with the exception of age in stratum three and parental education in stratum eleven. The pattern was very similar to that for the whole sample. The mean difference across all students in optional Transition Year schools was 1.7 grade points but this was reduced to 0.9 grade points when averaged across strata. Similarly, the unadjusted regression coefficient for Transition Year participation was 1.091 compared with 0.952 when averaged across the strata.

In sum, Transition Year participation appears to confer a performance advantage even when participants and non-participants are matched in terms of prior background, attitudes and performance.

Chapter Nine

CONCLUSIONS

INTRODUCTION

The number of students taking part in the Transition Year programme has grown significantly since the mid-1990s. However, little is known about the nature of the programme and its impact on the students who take it. This study sets out to address this gap in knowledge by drawing on large-scale surveys of schools and students around the country as well as on detailed case-studies of how Transition Year operates "on the ground" in seven schools. At the school level, it explores the reasons why schools decide to provide the programme, the content of Transition Year and how it is implemented, and teacher perceptions of its success. At the student level, the effect of participation in Transition Year on a range of student outcomes, including school drop-out, subject take-up, exam performance and transitions to higher education, is analysed. This chapter presents the main conclusions and policy implications of the study.

9.1 TRANSITION YEAR PROVISION

Transition Year is now one of a range of senior cycle options for schools and students with the result that students' choices and experiences within senior cycle depend on the school they attend. Transition Year is currently provided in the majority of second-level schools. However, the programme is less frequently provided in smaller schools and those serving working-class communities, reflecting both logistical constraints (in providing the programme for a small number of students) and the perceived suitability of the programme for the student intake.

The population of schools providing Transition Year has not been fixed over time. The number of schools providing the programme increased dramatically following the programme's restructuring. However, it is important to note that that a considerable proportion (44 per cent) of schools not currently providing the Transition Year have run the programme in the past and discontinued it. The main reason for dropping the programme was lack of student demand for a three-year senior cycle. Discontinuing the programme was more common in designated disadvantaged schools, small schools and schools in the vocational sector, reflecting school concerns about the sustainability of the programme in the face of low student demand and about the suitability of Transition Year for all students.

At present, students attending small schools and those serving more disadvantaged communities are less likely to have the chance to take Transition Year. In terms of equity, it is important that all students should be allowed to access the programme where they so choose. However, it should be acknowledged that many of these schools have "tried" the programme and felt it was not "for them". The challenge in policy terms is to widen the appeal of the programme to a broader set of schools, an issue that is taken up later in this chapter. It is also important that logistical constraints relating to school size do not adversely impact on the viability of the programme. Such logistical constraints are likely to come increasingly to the fore with the projected decline in student numbers within second-level education. It is important, therefore, that decisions on the future of the programme reflect judgements about the value of Transition Year rather than pragmatic considerations (such as student numbers) alone.

9.2 TRANSITION YEAR: "CONSCRIPTS" OR "RECRUITS"?

Schools vary not only in whether they provide Transition Year or not but also, when they do so, in whether the programme is offered on a compulsory or optional basis. In a quarter of the schools providing Transition Year all students take the programme. Transition Year is more likely to be compulsory in the coeducational secondary sector and more middle-class schools. The decision to make Transition Year compulsory on the part of schools was generally related to the desire to make the perceived benefits of the programme available to all students. Because of logistical constraints, when very small schools provide Transition Year, they are more likely to require all their students to take the programme.

In schools with an optional Transition Year programme, student preference was seen as the most important factor influencing access to the programme. However, there is evidence that some students, especially those with behavioural difficulties, may be discouraged from participating in the programme. The decision to offer the programme as an optional one reflects the perceived difficulties of having unwilling participants in the year group alongside a concern with maintaining the distinctive and flexible character of the programme.

9.3 WHO TAKES TRANSITION YEAR?

The profile of students taking Transition Year reflects the kinds of schools providing the programme, access policy within the school and students' own choices. As a result, taking part in Transition Year remains a minority experience with less than half of the senior cycle cohort taking the programme. Students who are from middle-class backgrounds, have higher educational aspirations and are younger than average are more likely to take part in Transition Year than other students. There is also evidence that students with less of an attachment to school life are not as likely to enter the programme. If Transition Year is seen as having positive benefits, therefore, any such benefits will accrue to students who are already more advantaged in terms of their socio-economic background and experience of school life. The extent to which Transition Year does impact on student outcomes is discussed below.

9.4 MANAGEMENT OF THE TRANSITION YEAR PROGRAMME

Schools appear to vary in the extent to which the Transition Year programme is a whole-school undertaking, in terms of whole-school planning as well as teacher involvement in the design and running of the programme. In some of the case-study schools examined, almost all teachers are involved in taking Transition Year classes whereas in other cases, involvement is limited to a smaller number of more interested teachers.

The role of the Transition Year Co-ordinator is pivotal in the successful design and implementation of the programme. However, there is a good degree of variation in the amount of time allocated to co-ordinators for their role and in the extent to which they are facilitated in having formal access to those teaching the programme (in the form of group or one-to-one meetings).

While all co-ordinators had received in-service training, only a minority of staff teaching Transition Year classes in the case-study schools had received any training relating to the programme. In some cases, Transition Year training appears to be a "one-off" occasion whereby staff are given in-service before, or at the time, the programme is introduced into the school with little input subsequently. This means that any such training is likely to be confined to the core group of teachers initially involved in the programme. The main constraint on accessing training is not the availability of in-service provision or lack of willingness on the part of teachers to take courses but rather the absence of time for participation in such training. It is recommended that schools be facilitated in allowing teachers to take part in in-service training related to the Transition Year programme; such facilitation would require additional resource allocation (such as additional time for teachers and substitute coverage) for schools. Broader access to such training is likely to help maintain and reinforce the mission of the programme as well as assist teachers in developing more innovative course content and teaching methods.

In overall terms, the main resource constraint on the effective management of the Transition Year programme within individual schools related to the lack of time. More time was seen to be needed for co-ordination, for meetings among teachers taking Transition Year classes and for in-service training. Moreover, the current timetabling structures within schools militate against the development of interdisciplinary courses, for example, in restricting opportunities for team teaching. A further constraint related to the absence of financial resources, in particular for funding activities and outings. It is recommended that teacher allocation and resource provision to schools should take account of the specific requirements of the Transition Year programme, allowing for the time to plan and develop the programme in response to the school's own needs. It is imperative that the associated costs do not play a part in a student's decision to take part in the programme. The need for additional financial resources is particularly important in more disadvantaged schools where it is not appropriate to expect students (or their parents) to fund specific activities.

9.5 CONTENT OF THE TRANSITION YEAR PROGRAMME

The majority of schools use Transition Year as an opportunity for students to sample subjects with students usually choosing their Leaving Certificate subjects late in the school year. Only a tiny minority of schools require their students to select their Leaving Certificate subjects before entry to the Transition Year, although this is somewhat more widespread in boys' secondary schools and schools with compulsory Transition Year. However, schools differ in the extent of choice within the programme, with a significant minority (30 per cent) of schools requiring all students to take the same subjects.

The majority (70 per cent) of schools provide a diverse programme, offering at least seven different subject areas to their Transition Year students, ranging from traditional academic subjects to personal development. However, some variation is evident between different kinds of schools with smaller schools being somewhat more constrained in the number of subject areas they can offer. The nucleus of the Transition Year programme tends to be comprised of six subject areas: academic subjects, cultural studies, sports, computer studies, work-related learning and civic/social studies. Third-level taster courses (that is, university-type academic courses), personal development courses and practical skills courses tend to be timetabled only in those schools providing very diverse programmes. It is recommended that schools should be facilitated, if necessary through additional teacher and resource allocation, to provide as diverse a Transition Year programme as possible.

Traditional academic subjects play a core role in the academic programme; an average of nine academic subjects are offered with Irish, English, Maths, languages, sciences and History/Geography included in the majority of Transition Year programmes. As well as making up a significant part of the Transition Year programme, academic subjects tend to be allocated more class time than other subjects. While schools cover a broad range of academic subject areas within Transition Year, subject provision is shaped by the overall ethos of the school and by teacher availability. The result is that the extent to which students can use the programme to sample different kinds of subjects depends on the school they attend. It is recommended that schools should be facilitated in allowing students to take academic subjects they may not otherwise have the opportunity to experience. This could be accomplished through inter-school cooperation in provision of some subjects (e.g. more practical subjects) and/or through the provision of in-service training for teachers to provide "modules" in subjects other than their main specialism.

While preparation for the world of work is an explicit part of the Transition Year mission, schools vary in the extent to which Transition Year students have timetabled or other organised sessions of career guidance. It is recommended that the allocation of guidance hours to second-level schools take adequate account of the core mission of Transition Year in facilitating long-term career choices. Work experience represents the main instrument for increasing career awareness with students taking part in work experience placements in almost all of the schools which provide Transition Year. However, the placement varies in its timing, duration and structure. An important distinction was evident between placements which involved "career sampling" (students trying out job areas they might like to enter in the future) and those involving "jobs" (where the placements resembled, or even overlapped with, part-time paid jobs outside school hours). It is recommended that, where possible, schools should encourage students to engage in "career sampling" placements in order to maximise students' longer-term career choices. In addition, students are more likely to benefit from work experience where they receive adequate preparation for their placement and there is follow-up to assess what students have learned from their experiences. It is, therefore, recommended that schools locate the work experience placement within a broader structured programme of preparation and evaluation. A more structured approach to work experience placements could have longer term advantages in fostering institutional linkages between schools and employers and may ultimately contribute to curricular innovation in the area of enterprise education.

9.6 DELIVERY OF THE PROGRAMME

The majority of teachers taking Transition Year classes in the case-study schools are found to use their lessons to reinforce basic skills in the subject area, introduce new topics and use a range of methods to approach the subject in a different way. However, a significant minority of teachers appear to rely on more traditional "chalk and talk" methods with a slightly greater prevalence of traditional methods among those teaching established academic subjects, especially Irish, English and Maths. Teachers were more likely to report using a diversity of teaching resources rather than methods per se. A minority of teachers used textbooks as the main resource within Transition Year classes but this was more prevalent among those teaching Irish, English, Maths or languages.

There is little evidence of interdisciplinary teaching in the case-study schools but a number of courses are interdisciplinary in character. This pattern is likely to reflect, at least in part, organisational barriers to teacher co-operation in course delivery such as time-tabling structures.

Transition Year places a strong emphasis on the *process* of learning, for example, by encouraging self-directed learning. However, schools and teachers vary in the methods of assessment used. Regular homework and formal exams were a more common feature of practice among teachers of traditional academic subjects than among those teaching "new" subjects. However, among many teachers, there was a greater emphasis on project-work and the assessment of student participation than would be evident with other year groups.

Transition Year represents a unique part of second-level education in requiring teachers to develop their own curricula and modes of assessment rather than following a nationally standardised syllabus with a terminal State examination. It is recommended that curriculum development skills among subject teachers should be enhanced through initial and in-service teacher training. In addition, schools and teachers should be supported in developing more innovative modes of assessment, perhaps through the dissemination of existing models of good practice.

In three of the seven case-study schools, students were grouped into their base classes on the basis of their academic ability. While ability grouping was felt by some teachers to facilitate a more appropriate pace of instruction, streaming for all subjects (including less academic sub-

jects) would appear to be counter to the spirit of the Transition Year programme. Furthermore, in keeping with previous national research across
different year groups (Smyth, 1999; Smyth et al., 2004), students allocated to the lower classes in Transition Year appeared to be more dissatisfied with the programme and disaffected with school (see below).

9.7 PERCEPTIONS OF THE TRANSITION YEAR PROGRAMME

A national survey of school principals indicated that they saw the Transition Year programme as broadly successful, especially in its impact on
personal and social skills development among students. However, there
was variation across school types in the perceived success of Transition
Year with designated disadvantaged schools, smaller schools and those
in the vocational sector somewhat less likely to see the programme as
effective. Interestingly, these are the kinds of schools which are over-
represented among schools who have discontinued Transition Year in the
past, indicating some tension around the provision of the programme in
certain school contexts. In addition, perceived success tended to be
greater in schools providing more diverse Transition Year programmes;
in particular, principals in schools providing students with exposure to a
greater range of subject areas saw the programme as being more successful in facilitating subsequent subject and career choices among students.

Within the case-study schools, school management and staff tended
to see Transition Year as successful in terms of its effect on personal-
social development and facilitating subject and career choices. There was
some variation between schools, and among teachers in the same school,
in their perceptions of the programme. While some teachers felt that
Transition Year should be provided for all students, there was a notice-
able current of feeling that the programme is "not for everyone", benefiting more motivated students to a greater extent.

Variation in student perceptions of the programme was also evident.
A number of students felt that Transition Year had exposed them to different experiences, provided a "break" after studying for the Junior Certificate and made them more mature. However, other students considered
the year to be a "doss" and "boring". Negative perceptions appeared to
be more prevalent among students who were not highly engaged in

school life, in particular among less academic students in schools where they were required to take Transition Year.

In general, positive perceptions among staff and students appeared to be related to a number of elements of good practice: a whole-school commitment to the programme; an effective co-ordinator with time to develop and maintain contacts with other staff members; a diverse programme, with activities and outings being seen as particularly important by students; and a more innovative approach to assessment which was consistent with the overall objectives of the programme. There was, however, a tension evident for schools in developing these aspects of the programme while at the same time maintaining a level of academic engagement among students, particularly those with lower educational aspirations.

9.8 STUDENT OUTCOMES

Students who take Transition Year differ in a number of respects from those who do not take the programme. It is important, therefore, to take account of these differences in looking at the effect of Transition Year on student outcomes. This study has explored the impact of participation in the programme on a range of student outcomes, including school dropout, subject take-up, exam performance and entry to third-level education, controlling for prior differences between participants and non-participants.

On average, students who took part in Transition Year achieved higher Leaving Certificate exam grades and were more likely to go on to higher education than non-participants, all else being equal. This pattern may reflect a number of aspects of the programme. Firstly, students receive greater exposure to the kinds of subjects they will take for the Leaving Certificate and it would be surprising if this did not have any positive effects on subsequent performance. Secondly, being a year older as such does not seem to enhance academic performance. However, the emphasis on self-directed learning and the perceived consequences of participation for maturity may enhance the study skills of students. Thirdly, previous research (Smyth, 1999) has indicated higher academic performance among students who have had positive interaction with teachers and a number of students in this study reported improved relations with teachers as a result of taking part in the programme.

However, the performance gains from participation were less evident among two particular groups of students. Firstly, students who took part in Transition Year were more likely to work part-time during senior cycle and, where their employment continued into their Leaving Certificate year, the negative impact of working tended to cancel out the performance gains associated with programme participation, at least for male students. Secondly, students in predominantly working-class schools where the programme was compulsory did not achieve higher Leaving Cert grades than their counterparts who had not taken part in the programme. Furthermore, students in schools where Transition Year was compulsory tended to have higher drop-out rates than those in other school types. It appears, therefore, that Transition Year may not be as successful in academic terms in contexts where a higher proportion of students are less engaged in school life and where they are unwilling participants in the programme. This finding is consistent with the disaffection expressed by some students in the group interviews (see above).

Participation in Transition Year appears to channel students, particularly boys, towards humanities and business courses within senior cycle and higher education. This may reflect the content of the programme, in particular the promotion of mini-companies and practical business activities in the course of the year. However, it is also likely to reflect the kinds of skills fostered through Transition Year, for example, the emphasis on interpersonal rather than practical skills.

A limitation of this study was the inability to capture the effects of Transition Year on those student outcomes whose promotion represents the primary objective of the programme, namely, personal and social skills development among students. The group interviews with students yielded useful insights into what students perceived to be the impact of the programme. However, a systematic study of the effects of Transition Year on the development of these "soft skills" would require a large-scale longitudinal study with measures of student development before entry to, and after exit from, the programme. Such a study could usefully be extended to cover other aspects of second-level education and other programmes. Given recent social and economic change in the Irish context, it would perhaps be timely to assess the impact of young people's educational experiences, broadly defined, not only on their academic outcomes but on their social and emotional development within school and beyond.

9.9 THE FUTURE OF TRANSITION YEAR

The Transition Year programme represents a good example of the potential for policy innovation within the Irish educational system. The programme was explicitly introduced to provide a broader educational experience for second-level students and to move away from a strong emphasis on terminal examinations. The Transition Year programme is, therefore, very different from much of the rest of second-level education. Schools can decide whether to offer the programme or not. Within broad guidelines, schools can determine the content of the Transition Year programme and the mode of assessment used (if any). There are no standardised syllabi so individual teachers devise their own curriculum for their subject and there is no nationally standardised form of assessment. The assessment of the operation of the programme in this study indicates the potential value of providing such flexibility in programme design and implementation at the school and teacher level.

A major concern, however, is that this flexibility results in variable content and quality of programmes across different schools. This study has indicated that the nature and perceived success of Transition Year vary markedly across schools. It is evident that a successful Transition Year programme requires a number of elements:

- A whole-school commitment to the programme;

- Time for co-ordination activities and for co-operation among staff teaching the programme;

- Diverse programme content, incorporating knowledge from a range of different subject areas;

- The provision of a structured exposure to the world of work;

- The use of more innovative teaching methods;

- The use of more innovative forms of assessment and accreditation;

- On-going evaluation and redesign of the programme.

These elements can only be put in place if they are facilitated at the system level. In particular, the programme requires the allocation of time for co-ordination activities (including teacher meetings), resources for activities and outings, and initial and in-service training for teachers to facilitate syllabus design and the use of more innovative teaching and assessment approaches.

Transition Year is found to have definite academic benefits for students and is thought by the majority of principals nationally to have a positive impact on student development. At present, some students, especially those from working-class backgrounds and/or with a weaker attachment to school life, do not access these benefits. The question remains, therefore, as to whether the benefits of the programme should be extended to all students by making the programme compulsory or, more generally, whether the lessons learned from the Transition Year experience can inform developments in other parts of senior cycle education.

Transition Year could be made compulsory either by having all students take a stand-alone programme on entry to senior cycle or by interspersing Transition Year "modules" within a three-year senior cycle programme. The advantage of a compulsory Transition Year programme (either stand-alone or module-based) would be that any benefits of the programme would be available for all students. Making the programme compulsory for all schools and students (including schools who have tried and then dropped the programme) may, however, militate against the innovative nature of the programme. The findings of this study would also indicate a possibility that such a change might increase early school leaving for at-risk students who are required to spend an extra year in full-time education. The challenge in such a scenario is to find a way to improve the programme in such a way as to maximise the retention of at-risk students. Previous research has found that subjects with a more practical orientation may provide a way of promoting student engagement with school life (see Smyth et al., 2004). There is potential, therefore, for integrating more traditional "vocational" subjects and incorporating more practical skills courses into the programme as a way of broadening its appeal to less academically oriented students. Furthermore, student input into the content of the programme and individual Transition Year courses or modules may give students a greater sense of ownership of the programme and enhance student engagement.

It is clear that, regardless of the future status of Transition Year as a stand-alone or integrated programme, either on a compulsory or optional basis, much can be learned from the experience of the programme for senior cycle education in general. In particular, aspects that could be taken up by other senior cycle programmes include the emphasis on project work and team work, the emphasis on non-examination based assessment, the diversity of programme content, the emphasis on personal and social skills development, the use of active learning methods, and the development of links with the workplace. Some of these elements are explicitly incorporated into the Leaving Certificate Applied programme and the link modules of the Leaving Certificate Vocational Programme. However, these elements have not to date been integrated into the Leaving Certificate (established) programme or, for that matter, into provision at the junior cycle level. The experience of the Transition Year programme indicates the potential for using more innovative teaching and assessment methods and for having greater flexibility at the school and teacher level in course design.

The future development of Transition Year is contingent on broader policy changes within senior cycle education. It is beyond the parameters of this study to suggest one solution to defining the place of the programme within broader senior cycle provision. However, the study has yielded a number of insights into the nature and impact of the programme which could usefully inform policy development in this area.

REFERENCES

Anfara, V.A., Brown, K.M. and Mangione, T.L. (2002). "Qualitative Research on Stage: Making the Research Process More Public", *Educational Researcher* 31 (7): 28–38.

ASTI (1992). *The Transition Year Option: A Teacher's Handbook*. Dublin: ASTI.

Brookover, W., Beady, C., Flood, P., Schweitzer, J., Wisenbaker, J. (1979). *School Social Systems and Student Achievement: Schools Can Make a Difference*. New York: Praeger.

CEB (1986). *Senior Cycle: Development and Direction*. Dublin: Curriculum and Examinations Board.

Conniffe, D., Gash, V., O'Connell, P.J. (2000). "Evaluating State Programmes: "Natural Experiments" and Propensity Scores", *Economic and Social Review*, 31 (4): 283–308.

D'Agostino, R.B. (1998). "Propensity Score Methods for Bias Reduction in the Comparison of a Treatment to a Non-randomised Control Group", *Statistics in Medicine*, 17: 2265–2281.

Deane, P. (1997). *The Transition Year: A Case Study in the Implementation of Curriculum Change*. M.Ed. Thesis, University of Maynooth.

Department of Education (1993). *Transition Year Programme: Guidelines for Schools*. Dublin: Department of Education.

Department of Education (1996). *Transition Year Programme 1994–1995: An Evaluation by the Inspectorate of the Department of Education*. Dublin: Department of Education.

Department of Education and Science (various years). *Statistical Report*. Dublin: Department of Education.

Doyle, E. (1990). "The Transition Year", in G. McNamara, K. Williams and D. Herron (eds.), *Achievement and Aspiration: Curricular Initiatives in Irish Post-Primary Education in the 1980s*, Dublin: Drumcondra Education Centre.

Egan, O. and O'Reilly, J. (1997). "The Transition Year Project", *Oideas,* Spring, pp.49–59.

Goldstein, H. (1995). *Multilevel Statistical Models.* London: Edward Arnold.

Gorard, S. (2002). "Can we overcome the methodological schism? Four models for combining qualitative and quantitative evidence", *Research Papers in Education*, 17 (4): 345–361.

Hannan, D.F., Smyth, E., McCullagh, J., O'Leary, R., McMahon, D. (1996). *Coeducation and Gender Equality: Exam Performance, Stress and Personal Development.* Dublin: Oak Tree Press/ESRI.

Ireson, J. and Hallam, S. (2001). *Ability Grouping in Education.* London: Sage.

Jeffers, G. (2002). "Transition Year Programme and Educational Disadvantage", *Irish Educational Studies*, 21 (2): 47–64.

McCoy, S., Smyth, E. (forthcoming). *At Work in School.* Dublin: The Liffey Press/ESRI.

McKenna, P. and O'Maolmhuire, C. (2000). *Work experience as an education and training strategy for the 21st Century.* School of Education Studies: Dublin City University.

Millar, D. and Kelly, D. (1999). *From Junior to Leaving Certificate: A Longitudinal Study of 1994 Junior Certificate Candidates who took the Leaving Certificate Examination in 1997.* Dublin: ERC/NCCA.

NCCA (1993). *Assessment and Certification in the Senior Cycle.* Dublin: NCCA.

NCCA (2002). *Developing Senior Cycle Education: Consultative Paper on Issues and Options.* Dublin: NCCA.

Shavit, Y. and Müller, W. (1998) *From School to Work: A Comparative Study of Educational Qualifications and Occupational Destinations.* Oxford: Clarendon Press.

Smyth, E. (1999) *Do Schools Differ? Academic and Personal Development among Pupils in the Second-Level Sector.* Dublin: Oak Tree Press/ESRI.

Smyth, E., Gangl, M., Raffe, D., Hannan, D.F., McCoy, S. (2001). *A Comparative Analysis of Transitions from Education to Work in Europe.* CATEWE Project, Final Report to the European Commission.

Smyth, E. and Hannan, C. (2002). *Who Chooses Science? Subject Take-Up in Second-Level Schools.* Dublin: The Liffey Press/ESRI.

Smyth, E. and Hannan, D.F. (2000). "Education and inequality", in B. Nolan, P.J. O'Connell & C.T. Whelan, *From Bust to Boom?: The Irish Experience of Growth and Inequality,* Dublin: IPA/ESRI.

Smyth, E., McCoy, S., Darmody, M. (2004). *Moving Up: The Experiences of First Year Students in Post-Primary Education*. Dublin: The Liffey Press/ESRI.

Teddlie, C. and Stringfield, S. (1993). *Schools Make A Difference: Lessons Learned from a 10-Year Study of School Effects*. New York: Teachers College Press.

Transition Year Curriculum Support Service (2000a). *Transition Year Survey on Co-ordination: Report on Findings*. Dublin: Transition Year Curriculum Support Service, Blackrock Education Centre.

Transition Year Curriculum Support Service (2000b) *Support Active Teaching and Learning: Project Work*. Dublin: Transition Year Curriculum Support Service, Blackrock Education Centre.